TEACHER'S PET PUBLICATIONS

PUZZLE PACK
for
The Glass Menagerie

based on the book by
Tennessee Williams

Written by
William T. Collins

© 2005 Teacher's Pet Publications
All Rights Reserved

The materials in this packet are copyrighted
by Teacher's Pet Publications, Inc.

These pages may be duplicated by the purchaser
for use in the purchaser's own classroom.

Copying any of these materials and distributing them
for any other purpose is a violation of the copyright laws.

© 2005 Teacher's Pet Publications, Inc.
www.tpet.com

INTRODUCTION
If you already own the LitPlan for this title, this Puzzle Pack will refresh your Unit Resource Materials and Vocabulary Resource Materials sections plus give you additional materials you can substitute into the tests. If you do not already have a complete LitPlan, these pages will give you some supplemental materials to use with your own plan. There are two main groups of materials: one set for unit words (such as characters' names, symbols, places, etc.) and one set for vocabulary words associated with the book.

WORD LIST
There is a word list for both the unit words and the vocabulary words. These lists show you which words are being used in the materials and the clues or definitions being used for those words. You may want to give students a word list with clues/definitions to help them, or you may want students to only have a word list (without clues/definitions) if you want them to work a little harder. Both are available for duplication. The word lists can also be your "calling key" for the bingo games.

FILL IN THE BLANK AND MATCHING
There are 4 each of the fill in the blank and matching worksheets for both the unit and vocabulary words. These pages can be used either as extra worksheets for students or as objective parts of a unit test. They can be done individually if students need extra help or as a whole class activity to review the material covered.

MAGIC SQUARES
The magic squares not only reinforce the material covered but also work on reasoning and math skills. Many teachers have told us that their students really enjoy doing these!

WORD SEARCH PUZZLES
The word search words go in all directions, as indicated on your answer keys. Two of the word search puzzles have the clues listed rather than the words. This makes the puzzle a little more difficult, but it reinforces the material better. Two word search puzzles have words only for students who find the clue puzzles too difficult.

CROSSWORD PUZZLES
Both unit and vocabulary word sections have 4 crossword puzzles.

BINGO CARDS
There are 32 individual bingo cards for the unit words and 32 individual bingo cards for the vocabulary words. You can use your word list as a "call list," calling the words at random and marking them off of your list as you go, or you could use the flash cards by cutting them apart and drawing the words at random from a hat (or box or whatever). To make a better review, you might ask for the definition and spelling of each word as you call it out–or you could call out the definitions and have students tell you the words they need to look for on the puzzle.

JUGGLE LETTERS
The vocabulary juggle letter game is intended to help students learn the spellings of the words. One sheet has the definitions listed on it as an extra help for students who need it or to reinforce the definitions if you choose to do so.

FLASH CARDS
We've included a set of vocabulary flash cards you can duplicate, cut, and fold for your students. Some teachers make a few sets for general use by the class; others make a set for each student. Some teachers duplicate them for each student and have the students cut & fold their own. You can cut out just the words and put them in a hat, have each student pick out one word and write the definition and a sentence for that word. Students then swap words and papers, with the next student adding a sentence of his own under the last one. You can have students swap as many times as you like. Each time the student will read the sentences written prior to his own and then add a sentence. You can cut out the words and definitions separately and play "I Have; Who Has?" Each student in the room draws a word and definition. The first student says, "I have (the name of the word). Who has the definition?" The student with the definition reads it then says, "I have (the name of the vocabulary word she has). Who has the definition?" The round continues until all words and definitions have been given.

Glass Menagerie Word List

No.	Word	Clue/Definition
1.	ACT	Play division
2.	AMANDA	Mother of Tom and Laura
3.	APARTMENT	Setting of the play
4.	BETTY	Jim's fiancee
5.	COFFIN	Tom feels as if he is in a nailed up one
6.	COLLEGE	Laura quit business ____
7.	CONTROL	Amanda wants to ____ Tom
8.	DANCE	Jim asks Laura to do this
9.	DAUGHTER	Laura to Amanda
10.	DINNER	Laura was too sick to eat it
11.	FAMILY	Amanda, Tom and Laura together
12.	FIRE	Laura slipped on the ____ escape
13.	GENTLEMAN	Amanda hopes for ____ callers for Laura
14.	GLASS	____ Menagerie
15.	INSTINCT	Tom thinks causes of human action come from this
16.	JIM	The gentleman caller
17.	KISS	Jim gives Laura one to make her realize she is pretty and appealing
18.	LAURA	She can't deal with the outside world
19.	LAWRENCE	Author of Tom's novel Amanda returned to the library
20.	MAGAZINES	Amanda sold these to make extra money
21.	MENAGERIE	Glass____
22.	MIND	Amanda thinks causes of human action come from this
23.	MOTHER	Amanda to Laura and Tom
24.	OVERBEARING	Adjective to describe Amanda
25.	ROSES	Jim called Laura Blue ____ by mistake
26.	SCENE	Act division
27.	SEAMAN	Tom has paid his dues to the Merchant ____'s Union
28.	SON	Tom to Amanda
29.	STAGE	Place where plays are performed
30.	SYMBOLS	Things that represent other things or have double meanings
31.	TEST	Laura became physically ill during her first speed ____
32.	TOM	He hates his job and wants adventure
33.	TRAP	'All pretty girls are a ____, a pretty ____'
34.	UNICORN	Symbol for Laura
35.	WILLIAMS	Author of The Glass Menagerie
36.	WINGFIELD	Laura's last name
37.	ZOO	Place Laura liked to go instead of school

Copyrighted

Glass Menagerie Fill In The Blank 1

_____

_____

_____

_____

_____

_____

_____

_____

_____

_____

_____

_____

_____

_____

_____

_____

_____

_____

_____

_____

1. Glass____
2. Amanda sold these to make extra money
3. Laura was too sick to eat it
4. Place Laura liked to go instead of school
5. He hates his job and wants adventure
6. Place where plays are performed
7. Jim gives Laura one to make her realize she is pretty and appealing
8. Adjective to describe Amanda
9. Laura's last name
10. Amanda wants to ____ Tom
11. The gentleman caller
12. Author of The Glass Menagerie
13. Amanda to Laura and Tom
14. Act division
15. Jim's fiancee
16. Laura to Amanda
17. Author of Tom's novel Amanda returned to the library
18. Tom thinks causes of human action come from this
19. Laura slipped on the ____ escape
20. Tom has paid his dues to the Merchant ____'s Union

Glass Menagerie Fill In The Blank 1 Answer Key

MENAGERIE	1. Glass ____
MAGAZINES	2. Amanda sold these to make extra money
DINNER	3. Laura was too sick to eat it
ZOO	4. Place Laura liked to go instead of school
TOM	5. He hates his job and wants adventure
STAGE	6. Place where plays are performed
KISS	7. Jim gives Laura one to make her realize she is pretty and appealing
OVERBEARING	8. Adjective to describe Amanda
WINGFIELD	9. Laura's last name
CONTROL	10. Amanda wants to ____ Tom
JIM	11. The gentleman caller
WILLIAMS	12. Author of The Glass Menagerie
MOTHER	13. Amanda to Laura and Tom
SCENE	14. Act division
BETTY	15. Jim's fiancee
DAUGHTER	16. Laura to Amanda
LAWRENCE	17. Author of Tom's novel Amanda returned to the library
INSTINCT	18. Tom thinks causes of human action come from this
FIRE	19. Laura slipped on the ____ escape
SEAMAN	20. Tom has paid his dues to the Merchant ____'s Union

Glass Menagerie Fill In The Blank 2

_____

_____

_____

_____

_____

_____

_____

_____

_____

_____

_____

_____

_____

_____

_____

_____

_____

_____

_____

_____

1. She can't deal with the outside world
2. Adjective to describe Amanda
3. Glass____
4. Tom to Amanda
5. He hates his job and wants adventure
6. Author of The Glass Menagerie
7. ____ Menagerie
8. Author of Tom's novel Amanda returned to the library
9. Jim gives Laura one to make her realize she is pretty and appealing
10. Amanda thinks causes of human action come from this
11. Jim's fiancee
12. Jim called Laura Blue ____ by mistake
13. Act division
14. Place Laura liked to go instead of school
15. Mother of Tom and Laura
16. Amanda wants to ____ Tom
17. Tom feels as if he is in a nailed up one
18. Laura became physically ill during her first speed ____
19. 'All pretty girls are a ____, a pretty ____'
20. Symbol for Laura

7
Copyrighted

Glass Menagerie Fill In The Blank 2 Answer Key

LAURA	1. She can't deal with the outside world
OVERBEARING	2. Adjective to describe Amanda
MENAGERIE	3. Glass____
SON	4. Tom to Amanda
TOM	5. He hates his job and wants adventure
WILLIAMS	6. Author of The Glass Menagerie
GLASS	7. ____ Menagerie
LAWRENCE	8. Author of Tom's novel Amanda returned to the library
KISS	9. Jim gives Laura one to make her realize she is pretty and appealing
MIND	10. Amanda thinks causes of human action come from this
BETTY	11. Jim's fiancee
ROSES	12. Jim called Laura Blue ____ by mistake
SCENE	13. Act division
ZOO	14. Place Laura liked to go instead of school
AMANDA	15. Mother of Tom and Laura
CONTROL	16. Amanda wants to ____ Tom
COFFIN	17. Tom feels as if he is in a nailed up one
TEST	18. Laura became physically ill during her first speed ____
TRAP	19. 'All pretty girls are a ____, a pretty ____'
UNICORN	20. Symbol for Laura

Glass Menagerie Fill In The Blank 3

_____

_____

_____

_____

_____

_____

_____

_____

_____

_____

_____

_____

_____

_____

_____

_____

_____

_____

_____

_____

1. Symbol for Laura
2. Tom thinks causes of human action come from this
3. ____ Menagerie
4. Things that represent other things or have double meanings
5. Play division
6. Tom feels as if he is in a nailed up one
7. Laura's last name
8. 'All pretty girls are a ____, a pretty ____'
9. Amanda to Laura and Tom
10. Act division
11. Amanda thinks causes of human action come from this
12. Jim's fiancee
13. Laura to Amanda
14. Laura was too sick to eat it
15. Setting of the play
16. Author of Tom's novel Amanda returned to the library
17. He hates his job and wants adventure
18. Author of The Glass Menagerie
19. Amanda hopes for ____ callers for Laura
20. Place Laura liked to go instead of school

Glass Menagerie Fill In The Blank 3 Answer Key

UNICORN	1. Symbol for Laura
INSTINCT	2. Tom thinks causes of human action come from this
GLASS	3. ____ Menagerie
SYMBOLS	4. Things that represent other things or have double meanings
ACT	5. Play division
COFFIN	6. Tom feels as if he is in a nailed up one
WINGFIELD	7. Laura's last name
TRAP	8. 'All pretty girls are a ____, a pretty ____'
MOTHER	9. Amanda to Laura and Tom
SCENE	10. Act division
MIND	11. Amanda thinks causes of human action come from this
BETTY	12. Jim's fiancee
DAUGHTER	13. Laura to Amanda
DINNER	14. Laura was too sick to eat it
APARTMENT	15. Setting of the play
LAWRENCE	16. Author of Tom's novel Amanda returned to the library
TOM	17. He hates his job and wants adventure
WILLIAMS	18. Author of The Glass Menagerie
GENTLEMAN	19. Amanda hopes for ____ callers for Laura
ZOO	20. Place Laura liked to go instead of school

Glass Menagerie Fill In The Blank 4

_____
_____
_____
_____
_____
_____
_____
_____
_____
_____
_____
_____
_____
_____
_____
_____
_____
_____
_____
_____

1. Laura's last name
2. Amanda hopes for ____ callers for Laura
3. Amanda thinks causes of human action come from this
4. Jim asks Laura to do this
5. Place where plays are performed
6. Laura became physically ill during her first speed ____
7. Amanda to Laura and Tom
8. Laura was too sick to eat it
9. Adjective to describe Amanda
10. Amanda wants to ____ Tom
11. Author of Tom's novel Amanda returned to the library
12. Laura slipped on the ____ escape
13. Jim called Laura Blue ____ by mistake
14. Jim gives Laura one to make her realize she is pretty and appealing
15. Amanda, Tom and Laura together
16. Play division
17. Author of The Glass Menagerie
18. Glass____
19. Laura quit business ____
20. Laura to Amanda

Glass Menagerie Fill In The Blank 4 Answer Key

WINGFIELD	1. Laura's last name
GENTLEMAN	2. Amanda hopes for ____ callers for Laura
MIND	3. Amanda thinks causes of human action come from this
DANCE	4. Jim asks Laura to do this
STAGE	5. Place where plays are performed
TEST	6. Laura became physically ill during her first speed ____
MOTHER	7. Amanda to Laura and Tom
DINNER	8. Laura was too sick to eat it
OVERBEARING	9. Adjective to describe Amanda
CONTROL	10. Amanda wants to ____ Tom
LAWRENCE	11. Author of Tom's novel Amanda returned to the library
FIRE	12. Laura slipped on the ____ escape
ROSES	13. Jim called Laura Blue ____ by mistake
KISS	14. Jim gives Laura one to make her realize she is pretty and appealing
FAMILY	15. Amanda, Tom and Laura together
ACT	16. Play division
WILLIAMS	17. Author of The Glass Menagerie
MENAGERIE	18. Glass____
COLLEGE	19. Laura quit business ____
DAUGHTER	20. Laura to Amanda

Glass Menagerie Matching 1

___ 1. MOTHER   A. Act division
___ 2. UNICORN   B. Laura to Amanda
___ 3. TRAP   C. Place Laura liked to go instead of school
___ 4. APARTMENT   D. Mother of Tom and Laura
___ 5. AMANDA   E. Place where plays are performed
___ 6. OVERBEARING   F. Symbol for Laura
___ 7. SCENE   G. Adjective to describe Amanda
___ 8. KISS   H. Tom thinks causes of human action come from this
___ 9. COLLEGE   I. Amanda wants to ____ Tom
___10. ROSES   J. Jim called Laura Blue ____ by mistake
___11. SYMBOLS   K. Jim asks Laura to do this
___12. DAUGHTER   L. Play division
___13. TEST   M. Amanda sold these to make extra money
___14. MAGAZINES   N. ____ Menagerie
___15. GENTLEMAN   O. Things that represent other things or have double meanings
___16. CONTROL   P. Amanda to Laura and Tom
___17. LAURA   Q. Laura was too sick to eat it
___18. GLASS   R. Setting of the play
___19. ZOO   S. Tom has paid his dues to the Merchant ____'s Union
___20. STAGE   T. 'All pretty girls are a ____, a pretty ____'
___21. INSTINCT   U. She can't deal with the outside world
___22. DANCE   V. Jim gives Laura one to make her realize she is pretty and appealing
___23. SEAMAN   W. Laura became physically ill during her first speed ____
___24. ACT   X. Laura quit business ____
___25. DINNER   Y. Amanda hopes for ____ callers for Laura

Glass Menagerie Matching 1 Answer Key

P - 1. MOTHER	A. Act division
F - 2. UNICORN	B. Laura to Amanda
T - 3. TRAP	C. Place Laura liked to go instead of school
R - 4. APARTMENT	D. Mother of Tom and Laura
D - 5. AMANDA	E. Place where plays are performed
G - 6. OVERBEARING	F. Symbol for Laura
A - 7. SCENE	G. Adjective to describe Amanda
V - 8. KISS	H. Tom thinks causes of human action come from this
X - 9. COLLEGE	I. Amanda wants to ____ Tom
J - 10. ROSES	J. Jim called Laura Blue ____ by mistake
O - 11. SYMBOLS	K. Jim asks Laura to do this
B - 12. DAUGHTER	L. Play division
W - 13. TEST	M. Amanda sold these to make extra money
M - 14. MAGAZINES	N. ____ Menagerie
Y - 15. GENTLEMAN	O. Things that represent other things or have double meanings
I - 16. CONTROL	P. Amanda to Laura and Tom
U - 17. LAURA	Q. Laura was too sick to eat it
N - 18. GLASS	R. Setting of the play
C - 19. ZOO	S. Tom has paid his dues to the Merchant ____'s Union
E - 20. STAGE	T. 'All pretty girls are a ____, a pretty ____'
H - 21. INSTINCT	U. She can't deal with the outside world
K - 22. DANCE	V. Jim gives Laura one to make her realize she is pretty and appealing
S - 23. SEAMAN	W. Laura became physically ill during her first speed ____
L - 24. ACT	X. Laura quit business ____
Q - 25. DINNER	Y. Amanda hopes for ____ callers for Laura

Glass Menagerie Matching 2

___ 1. MENAGERIE   A. Amanda wants to ____ Tom
___ 2. WINGFIELD   B. Amanda to Laura and Tom
___ 3. SEAMAN   C. She can't deal with the outside world
___ 4. TOM   D. Place where plays are performed
___ 5. CONTROL   E. The gentleman caller
___ 6. SYMBOLS   F. Setting of the play
___ 7. ROSES   G. Amanda sold these to make extra money
___ 8. AMANDA   H. Author of The Glass Menagerie
___ 9. LAWRENCE   I. Act division
___10. JIM   J. Amanda hopes for ____ callers for Laura
___11. FAMILY   K. He hates his job and wants adventure
___12. SON   L. Tom to Amanda
___13. LAURA   M. Mother of Tom and Laura
___14. KISS   N. Glass____
___15. APARTMENT   O. Laura slipped on the ____ escape
___16. OVERBEARING   P. Jim called Laura Blue ____ by mistake
___17. STAGE   Q. Adjective to describe Amanda
___18. FIRE   R. ____ Menagerie
___19. SCENE   S. Tom has paid his dues to the Merchant ____'s Union
___20. GLASS   T. Laura's last name
___21. WILLIAMS   U. Author of Tom's novel Amanda returned to the library
___22. MOTHER   V. Things that represent other things or have double meanings
___23. ZOO   W. Place Laura liked to go instead of school
___24. GENTLEMAN   X. Amanda, Tom and Laura together
___25. MAGAZINES   Y. Jim gives Laura one to make her realize she is pretty and appealing

15
Copyrighted

Glass Menagerie Matching 2 Answer Key

N - 1. MENAGERIE	A.	Amanda wants to ____ Tom
T - 2. WINGFIELD	B.	Amanda to Laura and Tom
S - 3. SEAMAN	C.	She can't deal with the outside world
K - 4. TOM	D.	Place where plays are performed
A - 5. CONTROL	E.	The gentleman caller
V - 6. SYMBOLS	F.	Setting of the play
P - 7. ROSES	G.	Amanda sold these to make extra money
M - 8. AMANDA	H.	Author of The Glass Menagerie
U - 9. LAWRENCE	I.	Act division
E -10. JIM	J.	Amanda hopes for ____ callers for Laura
X -11. FAMILY	K.	He hates his job and wants adventure
L -12. SON	L.	Tom to Amanda
C -13. LAURA	M.	Mother of Tom and Laura
Y -14. KISS	N.	Glass____
F -15. APARTMENT	O.	Laura slipped on the ____ escape
Q -16. OVERBEARING	P.	Jim called Laura Blue ____ by mistake
D -17. STAGE	Q.	Adjective to describe Amanda
O -18. FIRE	R.	____ Menagerie
I -19. SCENE	S.	Tom has paid his dues to the Merchant ____'s Union
R -20. GLASS	T.	Laura's last name
H -21. WILLIAMS	U.	Author of Tom's novel Amanda returned to the library
B -22. MOTHER	V.	Things that represent other things or have double meanings
W -23. ZOO	W.	Place Laura liked to go instead of school
J -24. GENTLEMAN	X.	Amanda, Tom and Laura together
G -25. MAGAZINES	Y.	Jim gives Laura one to make her realize she is pretty and appealing

Copyrighted

Glass Menagerie Matching 3

___ 1. LAWRENCE   A. Jim called Laura Blue ____ by mistake
___ 2. TOM   B. Laura was too sick to eat it
___ 3. UNICORN   C. Glass____
___ 4. TEST   D. Amanda thinks causes of human action come from this
___ 5. MENAGERIE   E. Symbol for Laura
___ 6. SEAMAN   F. Things that represent other things or have double meanings
___ 7. TRAP   G. Play division
___ 8. DANCE   H. Tom to Amanda
___ 9. ROSES   I. Amanda, Tom and Laura together
___10. APARTMENT   J. He hates his job and wants adventure
___11. WINGFIELD   K. Laura's last name
___12. JIM   L. The gentleman caller
___13. BETTY   M. Amanda to Laura and Tom
___14. COLLEGE   N. 'All pretty girls are a ____, a pretty ____'
___15. COFFIN   O. Laura became physically ill during her first speed ____
___16. MOTHER   P. Amanda wants to ____ Tom
___17. SON   Q. Amanda sold these to make extra money
___18. FAMILY   R. Setting of the play
___19. CONTROL   S. Tom feels as if he is in a nailed up one
___20. MIND   T. Tom has paid his dues to the Merchant ____'s Union
___21. ACT   U. Jim's fiancee
___22. MAGAZINES   V. Author of Tom's novel Amanda returned to the library
___23. INSTINCT   W. Jim asks Laura to do this
___24. DINNER   X. Laura quit business ____
___25. SYMBOLS   Y. Tom thinks causes of human action come from this

Glass Menagerie Matching 3 Answer Key

V - 1. LAWRENCE	A.	Jim called Laura Blue ____ by mistake
J - 2. TOM	B.	Laura was too sick to eat it
E - 3. UNICORN	C.	Glass ____
O - 4. TEST	D.	Amanda thinks causes of human action come from this
C - 5. MENAGERIE	E.	Symbol for Laura
T - 6. SEAMAN	F.	Things that represent other things or have double meanings
N - 7. TRAP	G.	Play division
W - 8. DANCE	H.	Tom to Amanda
A - 9. ROSES	I.	Amanda, Tom and Laura together
R - 10. APARTMENT	J.	He hates his job and wants adventure
K - 11. WINGFIELD	K.	Laura's last name
L - 12. JIM	L.	The gentleman caller
U - 13. BETTY	M.	Amanda to Laura and Tom
X - 14. COLLEGE	N.	'All pretty girls are a ____, a pretty ____'
S - 15. COFFIN	O.	Laura became physically ill during her first speed ____
M - 16. MOTHER	P.	Amanda wants to ____ Tom
H - 17. SON	Q.	Amanda sold these to make extra money
I - 18. FAMILY	R.	Setting of the play
P - 19. CONTROL	S.	Tom feels as if he is in a nailed up one
D - 20. MIND	T.	Tom has paid his dues to the Merchant ____'s Union
G - 21. ACT	U.	Jim's fiancee
Q - 22. MAGAZINES	V.	Author of Tom's novel Amanda returned to the library
Y - 23. INSTINCT	W.	Jim asks Laura to do this
B - 24. DINNER	X.	Laura quit business ____
F - 25. SYMBOLS	Y.	Tom thinks causes of human action come from this

Glass Menagerie Matching 4

___ 1. SCENE
___ 2. STAGE
___ 3. FAMILY
___ 4. MOTHER
___ 5. KISS
___ 6. OVERBEARING
___ 7. SYMBOLS
___ 8. FIRE
___ 9. AMANDA
___ 10. MENAGERIE
___ 11. TEST
___ 12. APARTMENT
___ 13. SON
___ 14. CONTROL
___ 15. BETTY
___ 16. DINNER
___ 17. ZOO
___ 18. GENTLEMAN
___ 19. WILLIAMS
___ 20. COLLEGE
___ 21. JIM
___ 22. WINGFIELD
___ 23. INSTINCT
___ 24. MIND
___ 25. ACT

A. Jim gives Laura one to make her realize she is pretty and appealing
B. Amanda thinks causes of human action come from this
C. Place Laura liked to go instead of school
D. Tom thinks causes of human action come from this
E. Setting of the play
F. Amanda wants to ____ Tom
G. Author of The Glass Menagerie
H. Laura was too sick to eat it
I. Mother of Tom and Laura
J. Jim's fiancee
K. Tom to Amanda
L. Laura became physically ill during her first speed ____
M. Laura's last name
N. Play division
O. Glass ____
P. Laura quit business ____
Q. The gentleman caller
R. Amanda, Tom and Laura together
S. Things that represent other things or have double meanings
T. Amanda hopes for ____ callers for Laura
U. Act division
V. Place where plays are performed
W. Adjective to describe Amanda
X. Amanda to Laura and Tom
Y. Laura slipped on the ____ escape

19
Copyrighted

Glass Menagerie Matching 4 Answer Key

U - 1. SCENE	A.	Jim gives Laura one to make her realize she is pretty and appealing
V - 2. STAGE	B.	Amanda thinks causes of human action come from this
R - 3. FAMILY	C.	Place Laura liked to go instead of school
X - 4. MOTHER	D.	Tom thinks causes of human action come from this
A - 5. KISS	E.	Setting of the play
W - 6. OVERBEARING	F.	Amanda wants to ____ Tom
S - 7. SYMBOLS	G.	Author of The Glass Menagerie
Y - 8. FIRE	H.	Laura was too sick to eat it
I - 9. AMANDA	I.	Mother of Tom and Laura
O - 10. MENAGERIE	J.	Jim's fiancee
L - 11. TEST	K.	Tom to Amanda
E - 12. APARTMENT	L.	Laura became physically ill during her first speed ____
K - 13. SON	M.	Laura's last name
F - 14. CONTROL	N.	Play division
J - 15. BETTY	O.	Glass ____
H - 16. DINNER	P.	Laura quit business ____
C - 17. ZOO	Q.	The gentleman caller
T - 18. GENTLEMAN	R.	Amanda, Tom and Laura together
G - 19. WILLIAMS	S.	Things that represent other things or have double meanings
P - 20. COLLEGE	T.	Amanda hopes for ____ callers for Laura
Q - 21. JIM	U.	Act division
M - 22. WINGFIELD	V.	Place where plays are performed
D - 23. INSTINCT	W.	Adjective to describe Amanda
B - 24. MIND	X.	Amanda to Laura and Tom
N - 25. ACT	Y.	Laura slipped on the ____ escape

Glass Menagerie Magic Squares 1

Match the definition with the vocabulary word. Put your answers in the magic squares below. When your answers are correct, all columns and rows will add to the same number.

A. FAMILY
B. APARTMENT
C. ZOO
D. LAURA
E. MOTHER
F. SEAMAN
G. DINNER
H. WINGFIELD
I. DANCE
J. INSTINCT
K. DAUGHTER
L. COFFIN
M. ROSES
N. GLASS
O. FIRE
P. JIM

1. Laura slipped on the ____ escape
2. She can't deal with the outside world
3. Tom thinks causes of human action come from this
4. Amanda to Laura and Tom
5. Jim asks Laura to do this
6. Tom has paid his dues to the Merchant ____'s Union
7. The gentleman caller
8. Place Laura liked to go instead of school
9. Laura's last name
10. Laura to Amanda
11. Amanda, Tom and Laura together
12. ____ Menagerie
13. Setting of the play
14. Jim called Laura Blue ____ by mistake
15. Laura was too sick to eat it
16. Tom feels as if he is in a nailed up one

A=	B=	C=	D=
E=	F=	G=	H=
I=	J=	K=	L=
M=	N=	O=	P=

Glass Menagerie Magic Squares 1 Answer Key

Match the definition with the vocabulary word. Put your answers in the magic squares below. When your answers are correct, all columns and rows will add to the same number.

A. FAMILY
B. APARTMENT
C. ZOO
D. LAURA
E. MOTHER
F. SEAMAN
G. DINNER
H. WINGFIELD
I. DANCE
J. INSTINCT
K. DAUGHTER
L. COFFIN
M. ROSES
N. GLASS
O. FIRE
P. JIM

1. Laura slipped on the ____ escape
2. She can't deal with the outside world
3. Tom thinks causes of human action come from this
4. Amanda to Laura and Tom
5. Jim asks Laura to do this
6. Tom has paid his dues to the Merchant ____'s Union
7. The gentleman caller
8. Place Laura liked to go instead of school
9. Laura's last name
10. Laura to Amanda
11. Amanda, Tom and Laura together
12. ____ Menagerie
13. Setting of the play
14. Jim called Laura Blue ____ by mistake
15. Laura was too sick to eat it
16. Tom feels as if he is in a nailed up one

A=11	B=13	C=8	D=2
E=4	F=6	G=15	H=9
I=5	J=3	K=10	L=16
M=14	N=12	O=1	P=7

Glass Menagerie Magic Squares 2

Match the definition with the vocabulary word. Put your answers in the magic squares below. When your answers are correct, all columns and rows will add to the same number.

A. GLASS
B. COFFIN
C. TRAP
D. FAMILY
E. LAURA
F. AMANDA
G. UNICORN
H. BETTY
I. MAGAZINES
J. TOM
K. DANCE
L. SON
M. TEST
N. MOTHER
O. OVERBEARING
P. WINGFIELD

1. Laura became physically ill during her first speed ____
2. Mother of Tom and Laura
3. Jim's fiancee
4. Adjective to describe Amanda
5. Tom to Amanda
6. 'All pretty girls are a ____, a pretty ____'
7. ____ Menagerie
8. He hates his job and wants adventure
9. Jim asks Laura to do this
10. Amanda, Tom and Laura together
11. Tom feels as if he is in a nailed up one
12. Amanda sold these to make extra money
13. Amanda to Laura and Tom
14. She can't deal with the outside world
15. Symbol for Laura
16. Laura's last name

A=	B=	C=	D=
E=	F=	G=	H=
I=	J=	K=	L=
M=	N=	O=	P=

Glass Menagerie Magic Squares 2 Answer Key

Match the definition with the vocabulary word. Put your answers in the magic squares below. When your answers are correct, all columns and rows will add to the same number.

A. GLASS
B. COFFIN
C. TRAP
D. FAMILY
E. LAURA
F. AMANDA
G. UNICORN
H. BETTY
I. MAGAZINES
J. TOM
K. DANCE
L. SON
M. TEST
N. MOTHER
O. OVERBEARING
P. WINGFIELD

1. Laura became physically ill during her first speed ____
2. Mother of Tom and Laura
3. Jim's fiancee
4. Adjective to describe Amanda
5. Tom to Amanda
6. 'All pretty girls are a ____, a pretty ____'
7. ____ Menagerie
8. He hates his job and wants adventure
9. Jim asks Laura to do this
10. Amanda, Tom and Laura together
11. Tom feels as if he is in a nailed up one
12. Amanda sold these to make extra money
13. Amanda to Laura and Tom
14. She can't deal with the outside world
15. Symbol for Laura
16. Laura's last name

A=7	B=11	C=6	D=10
E=14	F=2	G=15	H=3
I=12	J=8	K=9	L=5
M=1	N=13	O=4	P=16

Glass Menagerie Magic Squares 3

Match the definition with the vocabulary word. Put your answers in the magic squares below. When your answers are correct, all columns and rows will add to the same number.

A. LAWRENCE
B. LAURA
C. KISS
D. WINGFIELD
E. JIM
F. INSTINCT
G. UNICORN
H. TOM
I. MAGAZINES
J. ROSES
K. SON
L. DANCE
M. OVERBEARING
N. BETTY
O. FIRE
P. APARTMENT

1. Laura slipped on the ____ escape
2. Jim called Laura Blue ____ by mistake
3. He hates his job and wants adventure
4. Author of Tom's novel Amanda returned to the library
5. Laura's last name
6. The gentleman caller
7. Tom to Amanda
8. Jim's fiancee
9. Tom thinks causes of human action come from this
10. Jim gives Laura one to make her realize she is pretty and appealing
11. Adjective to describe Amanda
12. Jim asks Laura to do this
13. Amanda sold these to make extra money
14. Setting of the play
15. She can't deal with the outside world
16. Symbol for Laura

A=	B=	C=	D=
E=	F=	G=	H=
I=	J=	K=	L=
M=	N=	O=	P=

Glass Menagerie Magic Squares 3 Answer Key

Match the definition with the vocabulary word. Put your answers in the magic squares below. When your answers are correct, all columns and rows will add to the same number.

A. LAWRENCE
B. LAURA
C. KISS
D. WINGFIELD
E. JIM
F. INSTINCT
G. UNICORN
H. TOM
I. MAGAZINES
J. ROSES
K. SON
L. DANCE
M. OVERBEARING
N. BETTY
O. FIRE
P. APARTMENT

1. Laura slipped on the ____ escape
2. Jim called Laura Blue ____ by mistake
3. He hates his job and wants adventure
4. Author of Tom's novel Amanda returned to the library
5. Laura's last name
6. The gentleman caller
7. Tom to Amanda
8. Jim's fiancee
9. Tom thinks causes of human action come from this
10. Jim gives Laura one to make her realize she is pretty and appealing
11. Adjective to describe Amanda
12. Jim asks Laura to do this
13. Amanda sold these to make extra money
14. Setting of the play
15. She can't deal with the outside world
16. Symbol for Laura

A=4	B=15	C=10	D=5
E=6	F=9	G=16	H=3
I=13	J=2	K=7	L=12
M=11	N=8	O=1	P=14

Glass Menagerie Magic Squares 4

Match the definition with the vocabulary word. Put your answers in the magic squares below. When your answers are correct, all columns and rows will add to the same number.

A. WINGFIELD
B. APARTMENT
C. CONTROL
D. BETTY
E. ROSES
F. LAWRENCE
G. DAUGHTER
H. TRAP
I. MAGAZINES
J. SEAMAN
K. ZOO
L. SON
M. DINNER
N. UNICORN
O. GENTLEMAN
P. JIM

1. Laura was too sick to eat it
2. Author of Tom's novel Amanda returned to the library
3. 'All pretty girls are a ____, a pretty ____'
4. Amanda hopes for ____ callers for Laura
5. Tom to Amanda
6. Amanda wants to ____ Tom
7. Laura's last name
8. Tom has paid his dues to the Merchant ____'s Union
9. Place Laura liked to go instead of school
10. Jim's fiancee
11. Setting of the play
12. Amanda sold these to make extra money
13. Symbol for Laura
14. Jim called Laura Blue ____ by mistake
15. Laura to Amanda
16. The gentleman caller

A=	B=	C=	D=
E=	F=	G=	H=
I=	J=	K=	L=
M=	N=	O=	P=

Glass Menagerie Magic Squares 4 Answer Key

Match the definition with the vocabulary word. Put your answers in the magic squares below. When your answers are correct, all columns and rows will add to the same number.

A. WINGFIELD
B. APARTMENT
C. CONTROL
D. BETTY
E. ROSES
F. LAWRENCE
G. DAUGHTER
H. TRAP
I. MAGAZINES
J. SEAMAN
K. ZOO
L. SON
M. DINNER
N. UNICORN
O. GENTLEMAN
P. JIM

1. Laura was too sick to eat it
2. Author of Tom's novel Amanda returned to the library
3. 'All pretty girls are a ____, a pretty ____'
4. Amanda hopes for ____ callers for Laura
5. Tom to Amanda
6. Amanda wants to ____ Tom
7. Laura's last name
8. Tom has paid his dues to the Merchant ____'s Union
9. Place Laura liked to go instead of school
10. Jim's fiancee
11. Setting of the play
12. Amanda sold these to make extra money
13. Symbol for Laura
14. Jim called Laura Blue ____ by mistake
15. Laura to Amanda
16. The gentleman caller

A=7	B=11	C=6	D=10
E=14	F=2	G=15	H=3
I=12	J=8	K=9	L=5
M=1	N=13	O=4	P=16

Glass Menagerie Word Search 1

Words are placed backwards, forward, diagonally, up and down. Clues listed below can help you find the words. Circle the hidden vocabulary words in the maze.

```
D K W D J C A L Z T S H F N H V C R V S X
G J J X I K M K V B M T N I Z L O T J V Q
R M L L J N A I Y M A X N F R M L Y E N N
N R G M D A N C E W I N G F I E L D J S S
F V O J O S D E X M L N W O K I E A D I T
H T F B T T A C R H L L D C M B G D U H M
T P S I S T H S B C I L S A D E E Z S R G
F E N E C S O E N F W E F E S T A G E S A
R C G A F B V N R Z S Y G I D T P T A Y R
T N D D H W E I Q O L P P R V Y H N M M V
M E Z O O F R Z R K I S S E L G S E A B W
N R K V T C B A H Q F F F G U M O M N O R
F W J M B D E G C X W V G A Z H N T N L T
P A R T D Z A A L N M J D N Y G D R J S L
H L Q Y N W R M G A X Y Q E K N O A P W Z
F L J B S G I C P M S K V M Z C M P J L P
J B L O R T N O C N G S K R I G X A K L X
N B P H Y N G F H F E G H N S M F K P L Z
X L Q Q G D F V L X N G U Y X V B Y P Y P
K B M Q M L Z H L X T G M S W W Q H Q W L
F Q B F V T X Z K L L Y V J L Q G V B Z S
V J Z Y V P Y G N R E T Z S C L L M P S F
Y D G P G P V M D L M V K K D L Z J D X Y
Q K X F N H C W F D A P P Q N P P D Q P C
F M W C Z Y J W T R N P G Y K X B N W G V
```

'All pretty girls are a ____, a pretty ____' (4)
Act division (5)
Adjective to describe Amanda (11)
Amanda hopes for ____ callers for Laura (9)
Amanda sold these to make extra money (9)
Amanda thinks causes of human action come from this (4)
Amanda to Laura and Tom (6)
Amanda wants to ____ Tom (7)
Amanda, Tom and Laura together (6)
Author of The Glass Menagerie (8)
Author of Tom's novel Amanda returned to the library (8)
Glass____ (9)
He hates his job and wants adventure (3)
Jim asks Laura to do this (5)
Jim called Laura Blue ____ by mistake (5)
Jim gives Laura one to make her realize she is pretty and appealing (4)
Jim's fiancee (5)
Laura became physically ill during her first speed ____ (4)
Laura quit business ____ (7)
Laura slipped on the ____ escape (4)
Laura to Amanda (8)
Laura was too sick to eat it (6)
Laura's last name (9)
Mother of Tom and Laura (6)
Place Laura liked to go instead of school (3)
Place where plays are performed (5)
Play division (3)
Setting of the play (9)
She can't deal with the outside world (5)
Symbol for Laura (7)
The gentleman caller (3)
Things that represent other things or have double meanings (7)
Tom feels as if he is in a nailed up one (6)
Tom has paid his dues to the Merchant ____'s Union (6)
Tom thinks causes of human action come from this (8)
Tom to Amanda (3)
____ Menagerie (5)

Glass Menagerie Word Search 1 Answer Key

Words are placed backwards, forward, diagonally, up and down. Clues listed below can help you find the words. Circle the hidden vocabulary words in the maze.

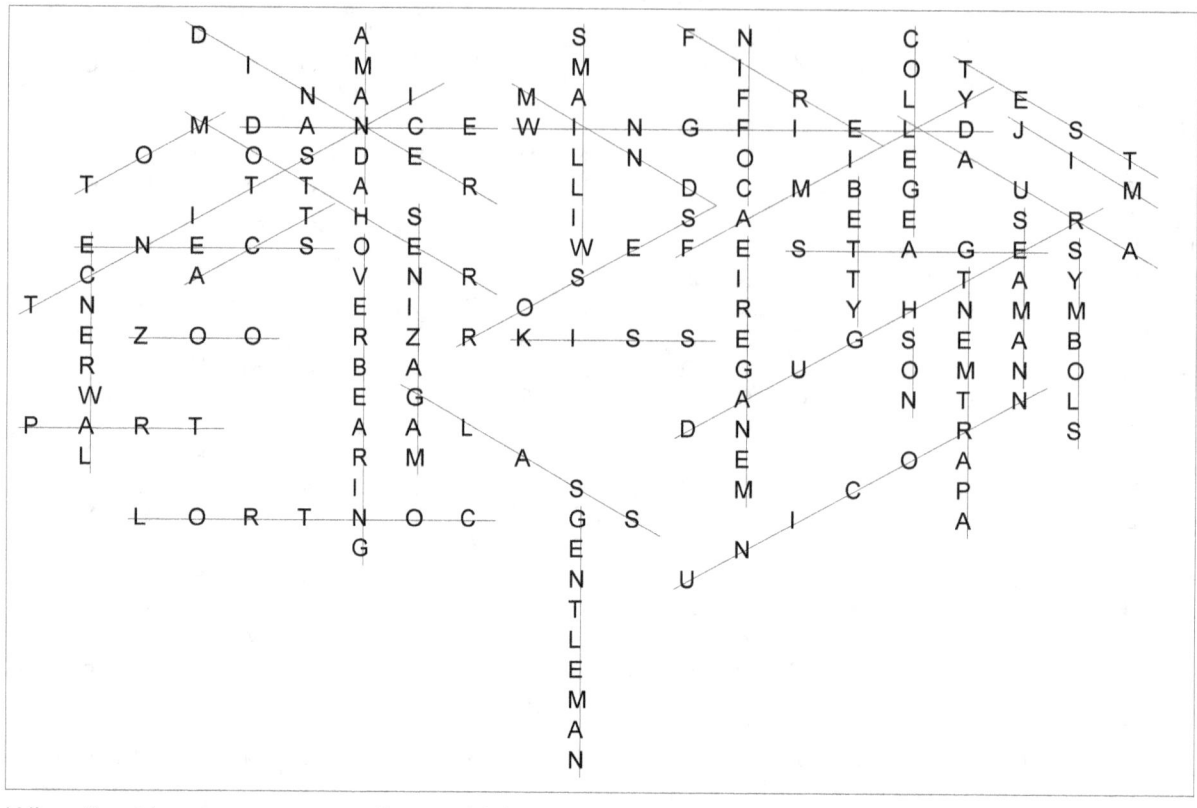

'All pretty girls are a ____, a pretty ____' (4)
Act division (5)
Adjective to describe Amanda (11)
Amanda hopes for ____ callers for Laura (9)
Amanda sold these to make extra money (9)
Amanda thinks causes of human action come from this (4)
Amanda to Laura and Tom (6)
Amanda wants to ____ Tom (7)
Amanda, Tom and Laura together (6)
Author of The Glass Menagerie (8)
Author of Tom's novel Amanda returned to the library (8)
Glass____ (9)
He hates his job and wants adventure (3)
Jim asks Laura to do this (5)
Jim called Laura Blue ____ by mistake (5)
Jim gives Laura one to make her realize she is pretty and appealing (4)
Jim's fiancee (5)
Laura became physically ill during her first speed ____ (4)

Laura quit business ____ (7)
Laura slipped on the ____ escape (4)
Laura to Amanda (8)
Laura was too sick to eat it (6)
Laura's last name (9)
Mother of Tom and Laura (6)
Place Laura liked to go instead of school (3)
Place where plays are performed (5)
Play division (3)
Setting of the play (9)
She can't deal with the outside world (5)
Symbol for Laura (7)
The gentleman caller (3)
Things that represent other things or have double meanings (7)
Tom feels as if he is in a nailed up one (6)
Tom has paid his dues to the Merchant ____'s Union (6)
Tom thinks causes of human action come from this (8)
Tom to Amanda (3)
____ Menagerie (5)

Glass Menagerie Word Search 2

Words are placed backwards, forward, diagonally, up and down. Clues listed below can help you find the words. Circle the hidden vocabulary words in the maze.

```
O V E R B E A R I N G A K W U D H C N X Q
V P D D Q W D K G D V Z P N R N K G J R H
Z J G R G G G J M F V P W A Y V I X N B T
R C P R K E X V P K L M R Z R N R C Y M G
I N S T I N C T Z S M L N T M T W R O P V
V D Y Z L T J V Z V H G G L H Q M N X R M
J Y R B Z L T J B V S Z T S Z D D E K M N
K B P K M E P Z G V S H V T N Z M K N J H
H M C Y L M J N R L M R X Q Q Y S Z V T H
M E F X F A X N Q P X Y T Q Q Y T D C G R
B N B P J N R J M Y B L H F B W J Y C P Q
T A B V V Q P G P N T J W P R I J X R Z H
L G J V F M Y W B G D M D C R L Z H Y M R
P E B R O S N L B H T R P Q V L C W F X S
T R B T W D O D V W V L R J Y I J F K S B
T I H E T R M A I J H L J D I A A L Y C F
H E G A T S E N I Z A G A M X M J M O T W
R Z S N N T G C Z X W U H W I S B L C P W
H Y O T W F Y E Q T G K F L R O L A G M T
Z C N J I R F C T H Y N Y C L E M I N D T
G B M E S O F F T R A N O S G N N P S H K
K L L S D S Q E R M A F Q E K E Y C V K P
Z D A M N E R H A H F P P H I C B M E K D
W O J S W S N E D I N N E R S S F I R E X
S N O S S S S R N L A U R A S A M A N D A
```

'All pretty girls are a ____, a pretty ____' (4)
Act division (5)
Adjective to describe Amanda (11)
Amanda hopes for ____ callers for Laura (9)
Amanda sold these to make extra money (9)
Amanda thinks causes of human action come from this (4)
Amanda to Laura and Tom (6)
Amanda wants to ____ Tom (7)
Amanda, Tom and Laura together (6)
Author of The Glass Menagerie (8)
Author of Tom's novel Amanda returned to the library (8)
Glass____ (9)
He hates his job and wants adventure (3)
Jim asks Laura to do this (5)
Jim called Laura Blue ____ by mistake (5)
Jim gives Laura one to make her realize she is pretty and appealing (4)
Jim's fiancee (5)
Laura became physically ill during her first speed ____ (4)

Laura quit business ____ (7)
Laura slipped on the ____ escape (4)
Laura to Amanda (8)
Laura was too sick to eat it (6)
Laura's last name (9)
Mother of Tom and Laura (6)
Place Laura liked to go instead of school (3)
Place where plays are performed (5)
Play division (3)
Setting of the play (9)
She can't deal with the outside world (5)
Symbol for Laura (7)
The gentleman caller (3)
Things that represent other things or have double meanings (7)
Tom feels as if he is in a nailed up one (6)
Tom has paid his dues to the Merchant ____'s Union (6)
Tom thinks causes of human action come from this (8)
Tom to Amanda (3)
____ Menagerie (5)

Glass Menagerie Word Search 2 Answer Key

Words are placed backwards, forward, diagonally, up and down. Clues listed below can help you find the words. Circle the hidden vocabulary words in the maze.

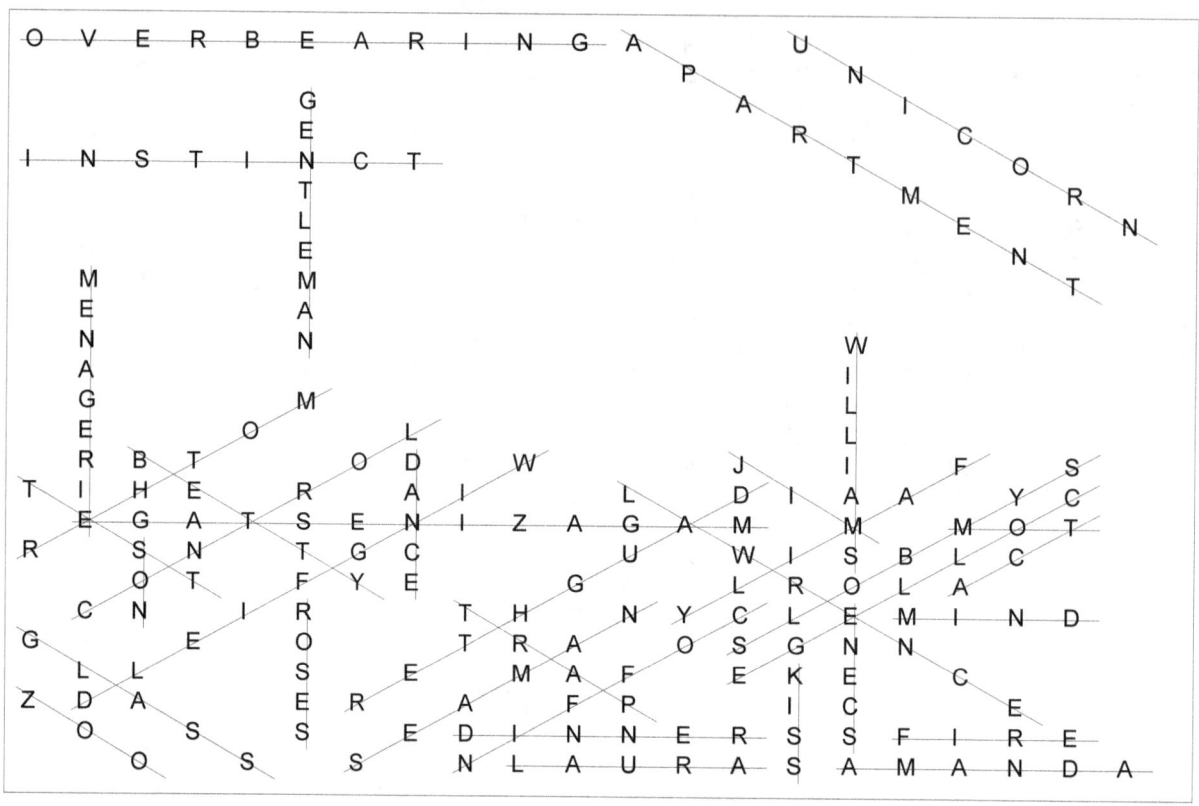

'All pretty girls are a ____, a pretty ____' (4)
Act division (5)
Adjective to describe Amanda (11)
Amanda hopes for ____ callers for Laura (9)
Amanda sold these to make extra money (9)
Amanda thinks causes of human action come from this (4)
Amanda to Laura and Tom (6)
Amanda wants to ____ Tom (7)
Amanda, Tom and Laura together (6)
Author of The Glass Menagerie (8)
Author of Tom's novel Amanda returned to the library (8)
Glass____ (9)
He hates his job and wants adventure (3)
Jim asks Laura to do this (5)
Jim called Laura Blue ____ by mistake (5)
Jim gives Laura one to make her realize she is pretty and appealing (4)
Jim's fiancee (5)
Laura became physically ill during her first speed ____ (4)

Laura quit business ____ (7)
Laura slipped on the ____ escape (4)
Laura to Amanda (8)
Laura was too sick to eat it (6)
Laura's last name (9)
Mother of Tom and Laura (6)
Place Laura liked to go instead of school (3)
Place where plays are performed (5)
Play division (3)
Setting of the play (9)
She can't deal with the outside world (5)
Symbol for Laura (7)
The gentleman caller (3)
Things that represent other things or have double meanings (7)
Tom feels as if he is in a nailed up one (6)
Tom has paid his dues to the Merchant ____'s Union (6)
Tom thinks causes of human action come from this (8)
Tom to Amanda (3)
____ Menagerie (5)

Glass Menagerie Word Search 3

Words are placed backwards, forward, diagonally, up and down. Words listed below are included in the maze. Circle the hidden vocabulary words in the maze.

```
G N W C I O D L G V T D C C Z H R K I S S
E V I O N V A Y A C D R B M O O X O G G V
N H N L S E U S A U J S A R K F O N S G V
T J G L T R G F W M R P F P H S F J Z E R
L V F E I B H K I E C A H J G M S I K H S
E J I G N E T H L N B D D N V Q B M N U G
M K E E C A E C L A B R B L L Q S Y N M V
A Q L T T R V I G F A M I L Y M I N D S
N T D F T I G Z A E G V C K Q L C Y T L L
Q X Q X M N H R M R D V A V H O G W Y Q N
V M T L W G B C S I Y G J P R G R W X Z V
X S S H G H Y W B E J C T N A P Z Q B C N
W H V J G Q B W N H W Y C K J R T G R W X
P M G Q M X V L S G L B F X Z Z T M F G N
J W F S X J M E F B N N W B V Q V M R R C
B W F P V C N S R G F X R Q D Z S P E S O
D P F T S I Q P J G Q E H F B Q S Y G N N
N A B D Z P J S T L H E C N E R W A L H T
R W N A Y J D T M T Q W R T T E L F A V R
X N G C R D A O O H B H L K T N Q Z S F O
N A M A E S Y M B O L S N L Y N T E S T L
M C V G R R N V A G V O C F R I H X J C V
H Y A Q I B T J C N S B P E R D Q Y W T H
X T D T F S C P Y K D P G H N B Q S Q Y H
S H Y D K V F Q K T L A D Z G E J H T C J
```

ACT	FAMILY	MENAGERIE	TEST
AMANDA	FIRE	MIND	TOM
APARTMENT	GENTLEMAN	MOTHER	TRAP
BETTY	GLASS	OVERBEARING	UNICORN
COFFIN	INSTINCT	ROSES	WILLIAMS
COLLEGE	JIM	SCENE	WINGFIELD
CONTROL	KISS	SEAMAN	ZOO
DANCE	LAURA	SON	
DAUGHTER	LAWRENCE	STAGE	
DINNER	MAGAZINES	SYMBOLS	

Glass Menagerie Word Search 3 Answer Key

Words are placed backwards, forward, diagonally, up and down. Words listed below are included in the maze. Circle the hidden vocabulary words in the maze.

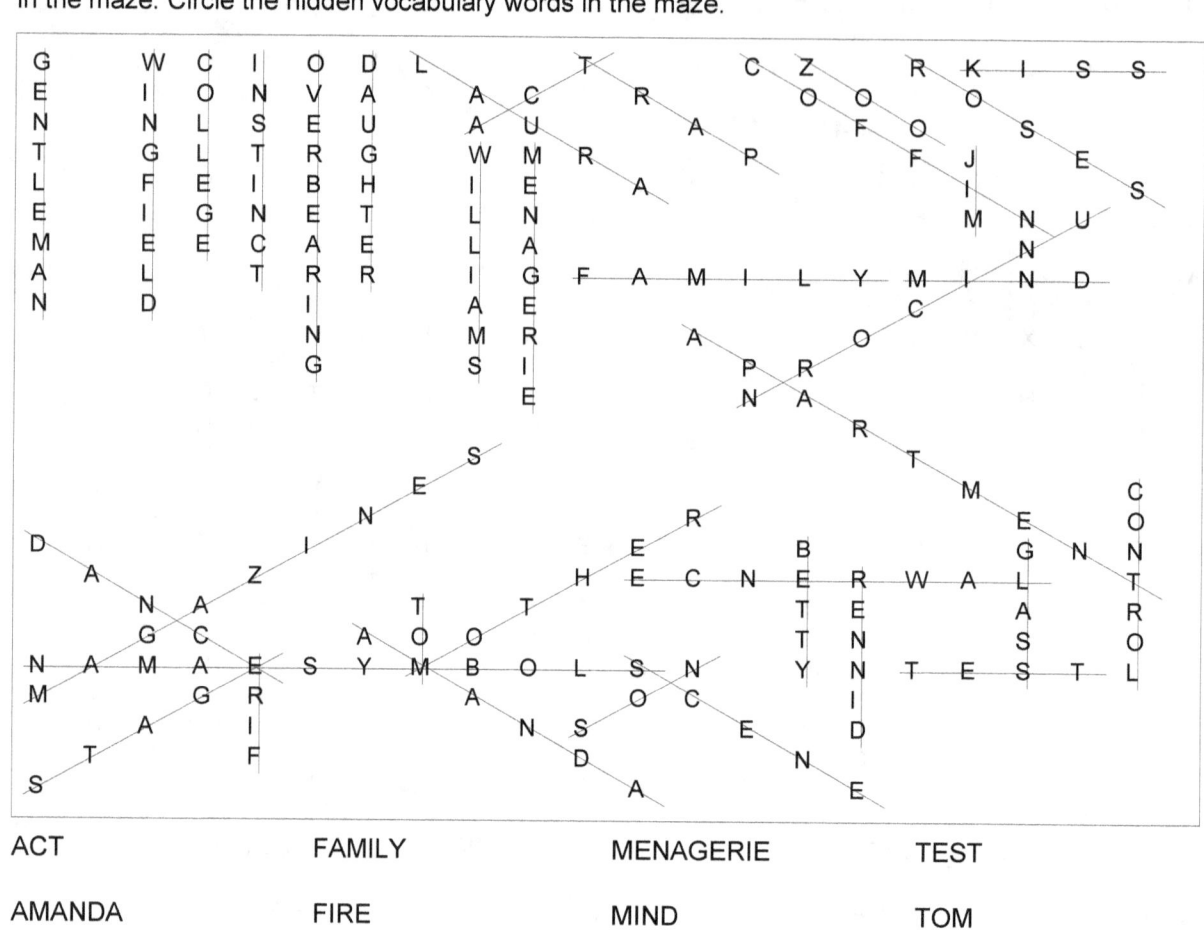

ACT	FAMILY	MENAGERIE	TEST
AMANDA	FIRE	MIND	TOM
APARTMENT	GENTLEMAN	MOTHER	TRAP
BETTY	GLASS	OVERBEARING	UNICORN
COFFIN	INSTINCT	ROSES	WILLIAMS
COLLEGE	JIM	SCENE	WINGFIELD
CONTROL	KISS	SEAMAN	ZOO
DANCE	LAURA	SON	
DAUGHTER	LAWRENCE	STAGE	
DINNER	MAGAZINES	SYMBOLS	

Glass Menagerie Word Search 4

Words are placed backwards, forward, diagonally, up and down. Words listed below are included in the maze. Circle the hidden vocabulary words in the maze.

```
L A W R E N C E C O N T R O L G D F R W R
P S N S G G X F L O Z C R V D E I I O I N
M R N V C G N U Z G F L F A T N N R S N N
J O T P V B B B N N W F S M P T N E E G J
E Y T P M S S M A I L L I W V L E B S F P
C L X H S M Y X P R C S T N Z E R E G I Z
N W A A E V B P A A P O P W M M S T Q E R
A G L U C R L P R E T Y R F H A O T B L Y
D G G W R B R B T B W Y J N H N N Y D M
V A Z M M A M R M R S J I K D D S R Y X R
H X U K M Z H Q E E Z X M H H Q R D M Q C
P X R G R P M S N V P D R T C G B X C J H
S W T L H N N Q T O X R G Y X K L P M K Q
H Z D D D T R J N G L Z R T V S X V S K K
R N X X F Y E V W K Z P S F W P W V N D X
B H T Z Z L C R D F Z C F E M Y Q W B N Z
Z Y B B T V W R X Y W K I D M S G Y N C H
T W Y W X Y Z K G N M R H J S R A K C C G
R M H J S B S F G T E M C G M S M Q B T Q
Q C S H B K A T L G C Y P M G L A C L N N
C Q Q C L M T Q A C V P E R R N Y A H T
V S B Z I T S N K G J N D T C R D M C S B
C O L L E G E M I S E N I Z A G A M A B H
K V Y L R M T O S C P X B V O E K R J C T
I N S T I N C T S Y M B O L S O M I N D T
```

ACT	FAMILY	MENAGERIE	TEST
AMANDA	FIRE	MIND	TOM
APARTMENT	GENTLEMAN	MOTHER	TRAP
BETTY	GLASS	OVERBEARING	UNICORN
COFFIN	INSTINCT	ROSES	WILLIAMS
COLLEGE	JIM	SCENE	WINGFIELD
CONTROL	KISS	SEAMAN	ZOO
DANCE	LAURA	SON	
DAUGHTER	LAWRENCE	STAGE	
DINNER	MAGAZINES	SYMBOLS	

Glass Menagerie Word Search 4 Answer Key

Words are placed backwards, forward, diagonally, up and down. Words listed below are included in the maze. Circle the hidden vocabulary words in the maze.

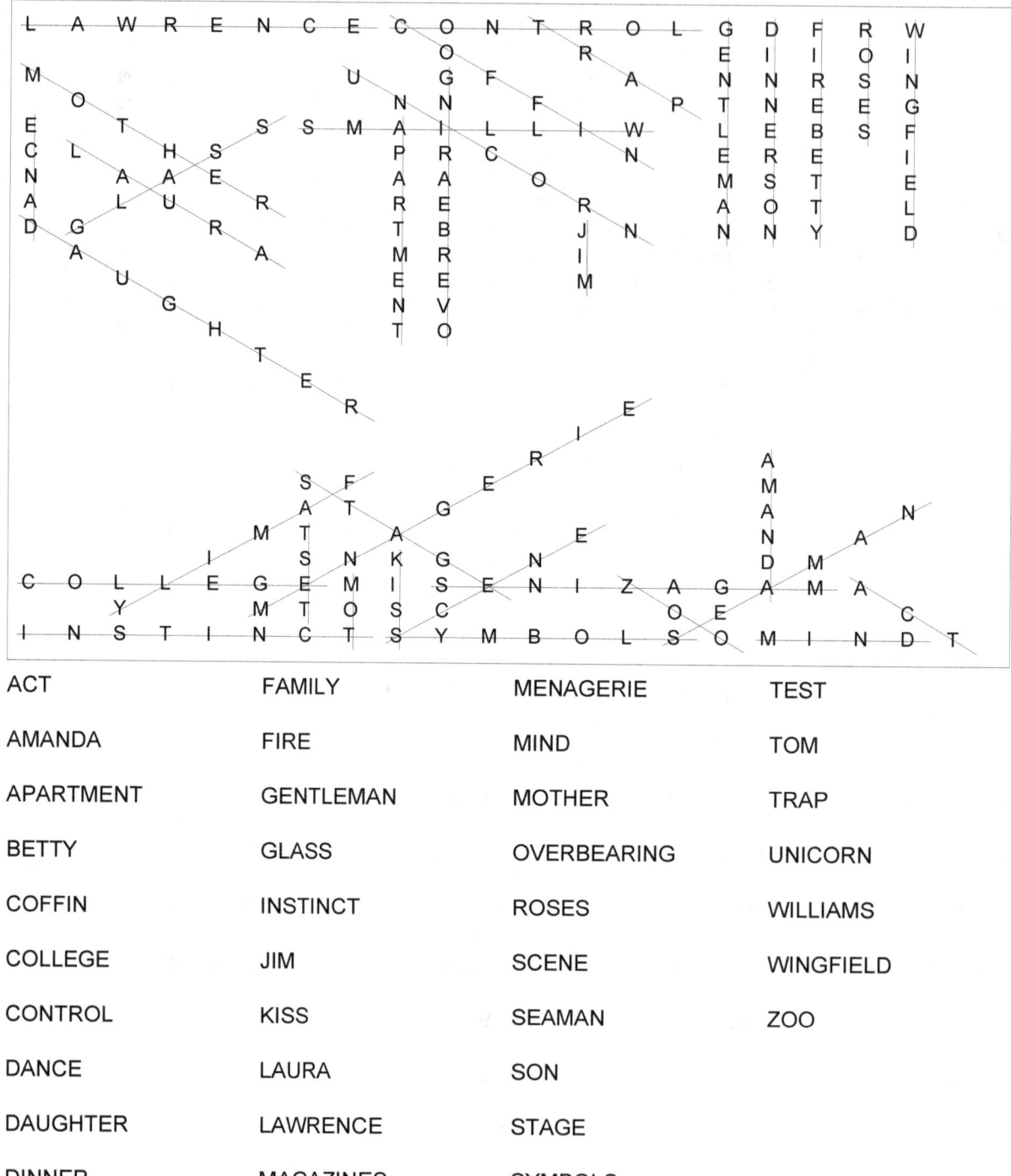

ACT	FAMILY	MENAGERIE	TEST
AMANDA	FIRE	MIND	TOM
APARTMENT	GENTLEMAN	MOTHER	TRAP
BETTY	GLASS	OVERBEARING	UNICORN
COFFIN	INSTINCT	ROSES	WILLIAMS
COLLEGE	JIM	SCENE	WINGFIELD
CONTROL	KISS	SEAMAN	ZOO
DANCE	LAURA	SON	
DAUGHTER	LAWRENCE	STAGE	
DINNER	MAGAZINES	SYMBOLS	

Glass Menagerie Crossword 1

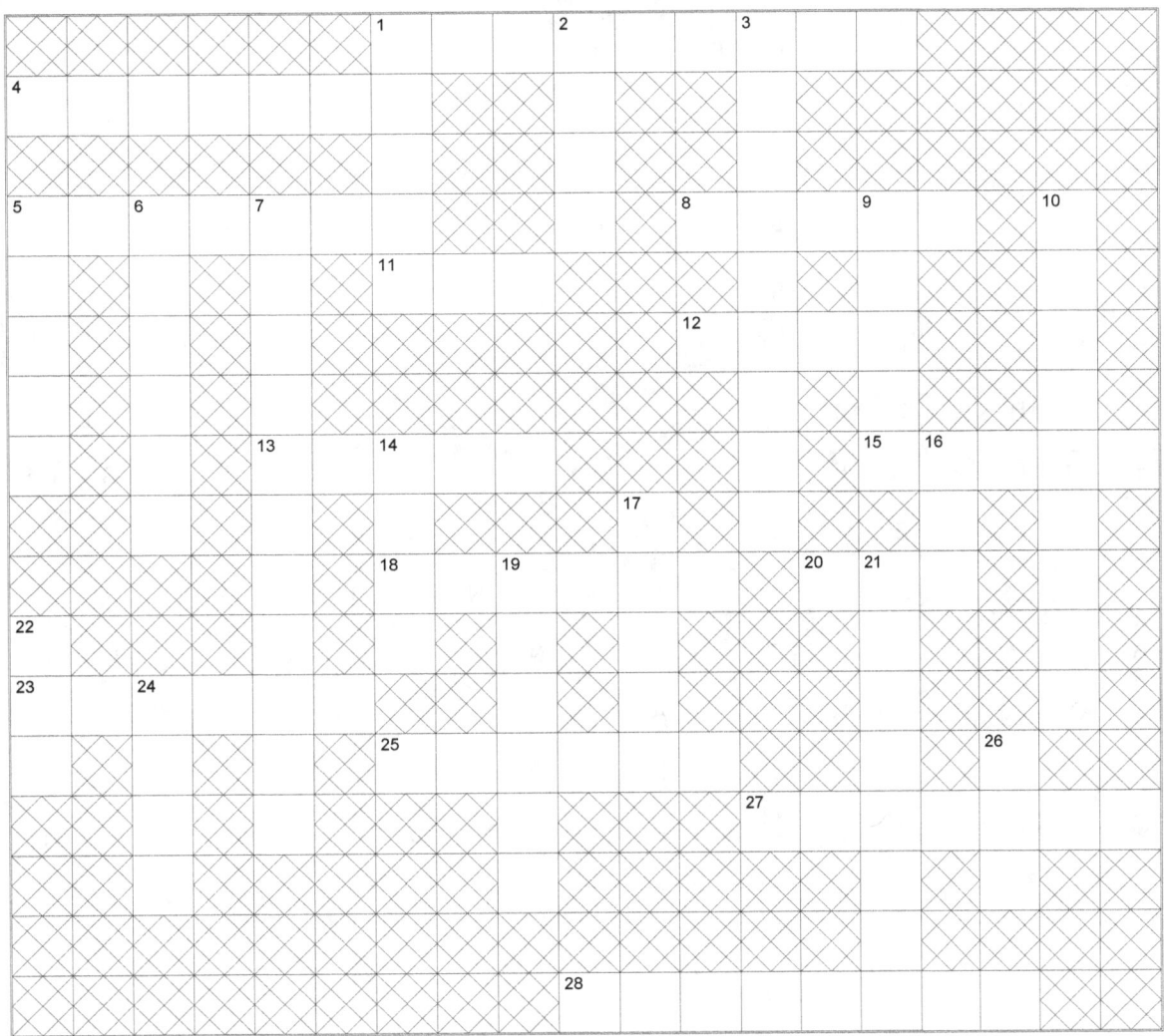

Across
1. Amanda hopes for ____ callers for Laura
4. Amanda wants to ____ Tom
5. Things that represent other things or have double meanings
8. She can't deal with the outside world
11. Tom to Amanda
12. Jim gives Laura one to make her realize she is pretty and appealing
13. Jim's fiancee
15. Place where plays are performed
18. Tom has paid his dues to the Merchant ____'s Union
20. The gentleman caller
23. Tom feels as if he is in a nailed up one
25. Laura was too sick to eat it
27. Symbol for Laura
28. Laura to Amanda

Down
1. ____ Menagerie
2. 'All pretty girls are a ____, a pretty ____'
3. Amanda sold these to make extra money
5. Act division
6. Amanda to Laura and Tom
7. Adjective to describe Amanda
9. Jim called Laura Blue ____ by mistake
10. Glass____
14. Laura became physically ill during her first speed ____
16. He hates his job and wants adventure
17. Jim asks Laura to do this
19. Mother of Tom and Laura
21. Tom thinks causes of human action come from this
22. Play division
24. Laura slipped on the ____ escape
26. Place Laura liked to go instead of school

Glass Menagerie Crossword 1 Answer Key

						¹G	E	²N	T	³L	E	M	A	N	
⁴C	O	N	T	R	O	L		R		E		A			
						A		A		G					
⁵S	⁶Y	⁷M	B	O	L	S		⁸P		⁹L	A	U	R	A	¹⁰M
C	O	V		¹¹S	O	N		Z		O					E
E	T	E					¹²K	I	S	S					N
N	H	R						N		E					A
E	E	¹³B	E	¹⁴T	T	Y				¹⁵S	¹⁶T	A	G	E	
	R	E		E			¹⁷D		S		O			E	
		A		¹⁸S	¹⁹E	A	M	A	N		²⁰J	²¹I	M		R
²²A		R		T	M		N				N			I	
²³C	²⁴O	F	F	I	N		A		C		S			²⁶Z	E
T	I	N		²⁵D	I	N	N	E	R		T				
	R	G			D				²⁷U	N	I	C	O	R	N
	E				A						N	O			
											C				
						²⁸D	A	U	G	H	T	E	R		

Across
1. Amanda hopes for ____ callers for Laura
4. Amanda wants to ____ Tom
5. Things that represent other things or have double meanings
8. She can't deal with the outside world
11. Tom to Amanda
12. Jim gives Laura one to make her realize she is pretty and appealing
13. Jim's fiancee
15. Place where plays are performed
18. Tom has paid his dues to the Merchant ____'s Union
20. The gentleman caller
23. Tom feels as if he is in a nailed up one
25. Laura was too sick to eat it
27. Symbol for Laura
28. Laura to Amanda

Down
1. ____ Menagerie
2. 'All pretty girls are a ____, a pretty ____'
3. Amanda sold these to make extra money
5. Act division
6. Amanda to Laura and Tom
7. Adjective to describe Amanda
9. Jim called Laura Blue ____ by mistake
10. Glass____
14. Laura became physically ill during her first speed ____
16. He hates his job and wants adventure
17. Jim asks Laura to do this
19. Mother of Tom and Laura
21. Tom thinks causes of human action come from this
22. Play division
24. Laura slipped on the ____ escape
26. Place Laura liked to go instead of school

Glass Menagerie Crossword 2

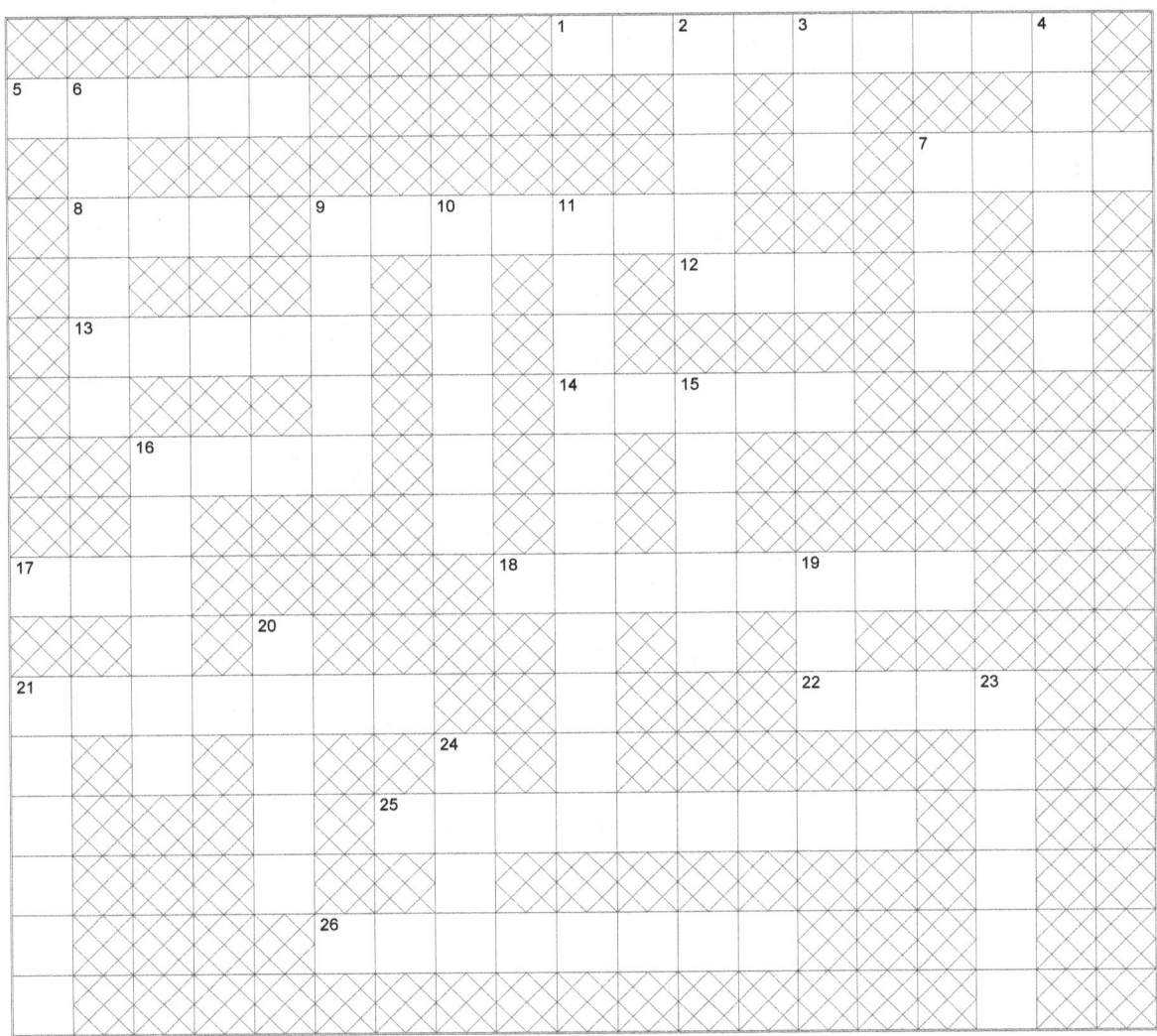

Across
1. Amanda sold these to make extra money
5. She can't deal with the outside world
7. 'All pretty girls are a ____, a pretty ____'
8. Play division
9. Things that represent other things or have double meanings
12. Tom to Amanda
13. Jim asks Laura to do this
14. Jim called Laura Blue ____ by mistake
16. Laura slipped on the ____ escape
17. The gentleman caller
18. Laura to Amanda
21. Laura quit business ____
22. Amanda thinks causes of human action come from this
25. Laura's last name
26. Tom thinks causes of human action come from this

Down
2. ____ Menagerie
3. Place Laura liked to go instead of school
4. Tom has paid his dues to the Merchant ____'s Union
6. Mother of Tom and Laura
7. Laura became physically ill during her first speed ____
9. Act division
10. Amanda to Laura and Tom
11. Adjective to describe Amanda
15. Place where plays are performed
16. Amanda, Tom and Laura together
19. He hates his job and wants adventure
20. Jim's fiancee
21. Tom feels as if he is in a nailed up one
23. Laura was too sick to eat it
24. Jim gives Laura one to make her realize she is pretty and appealing

Glass Menagerie Crossword 2 Answer Key

								1 M	2 A	3 G	A	Z	I	4 N	E	S
	5 L	6 A	U	R	A					L		O			E	
		M								A		O		7 T	R	A	P
		8 A	C	T		9 S	Y	10 M	B	11 O	L	S			E		M
		N				C		O		V		12 S	O	N		S	A
		13 D	A	N	C	E		T		E						T	N
		A				N		H		14 R	O	15 S	E	S			
			16 F	I	R	E		E		B		T					
			A					R		E		A					
	17 J	I	M					18 D	A	U	G	H	T	19 E	R		
			I		20 B			R		E		O					
21 C	O	L	L	E	G	E		I				22 M	I	N	23 D		
O			Y		T		24 K		N						I		
F					T		25 W	I	N	G	F	I	E	L	D		
F					Y			S							N		
I				26 I	N	S	T	I	N	C	T				E		
N															R		

Across
1. Amanda sold these to make extra money
5. She can't deal with the outside world
7. 'All pretty girls are a ____, a pretty ____'
8. Play division
9. Things that represent other things or have double meanings
12. Tom to Amanda
13. Jim asks Laura to do this
14. Jim called Laura Blue ____ by mistake
16. Laura slipped on the ____ escape
17. The gentleman caller
18. Laura to Amanda
21. Laura quit business ____
22. Amanda thinks causes of human action come from this
25. Laura's last name
26. Tom thinks causes of human action come from this

Down
2. ____ Menagerie
3. Place Laura liked to go instead of school
4. Tom has paid his dues to the Merchant ____'s Union
6. Mother of Tom and Laura
7. Laura became physically ill during her first speed ____
9. Act division
10. Amanda to Laura and Tom
11. Adjective to describe Amanda
15. Place where plays are performed
16. Amanda, Tom and Laura together
19. He hates his job and wants adventure
20. Jim's fiancee
21. Tom feels as if he is in a nailed up one
23. Laura was too sick to eat it
24. Jim gives Laura one to make her realize she is pretty and appealing

Glass Menagerie Crossword 3

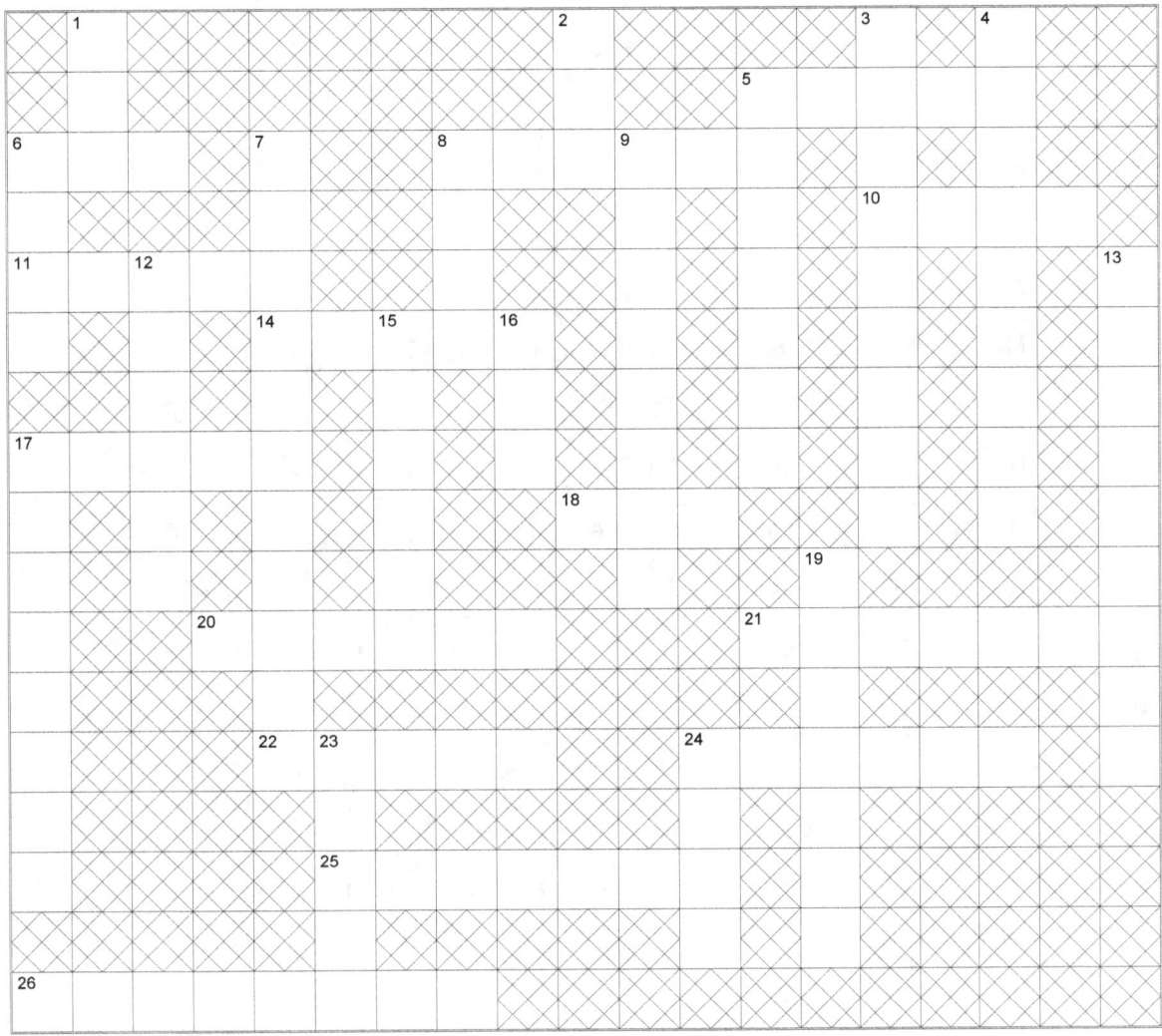

Across
5. Act division
6. He hates his job and wants adventure
8. Amanda, Tom and Laura together
10. 'All pretty girls are a ____, a pretty ____'
11. Place where plays are performed
14. Jim called Laura Blue ____ by mistake
17. Jim asks Laura to do this
18. Play division
20. Laura was too sick to eat it
21. Laura quit business ____
22. ____ Menagerie
24. Amanda to Laura and Tom
25. Symbol for Laura
26. Author of The Glass Menagerie

Down
1. Place Laura liked to go instead of school
2. The gentleman caller
3. Amanda hopes for ____ callers for Laura
4. Glass____
5. Things that represent other things or have double meanings
6. Laura became physically ill during her first speed ____
7. Adjective to describe Amanda
8. Laura slipped on the ____ escape
9. Tom thinks causes of human action come from this
12. Mother of Tom and Laura
13. Setting of the play
15. Tom has paid his dues to the Merchant ____'s Union
16. Tom to Amanda
17. Laura to Amanda
19. Amanda wants to ____ Tom
23. She can't deal with the outside world
24. Amanda thinks causes of human action come from this

Glass Menagerie Crossword 3 Answer Key

	1 Z		2 J		3 G	4 M
	O		I	5 S C E N E		
6 T O M	7 O	8 F A M	9 I L Y	N	N
E	V	I	N	M	10 T R A P
11 S T 12 A G E	R	S	B	L	G	13 A
T M	14 R 15 O S 16 E S	T	O	E	E	P
A	B	E	O	I	L	M	R	A
17 D A N C E	A	N	N	S	A	I	R
A	D	A	M	18 A C T		N	E	T
U	A	R	A	T	19 C		M
G	20 D I N N E R		21 C O L L E G E
H	N			N		N
T	22 G 23 L A S S	24 M O T H E R	T
E	A		I	R
R	25 U N I C O R N	O
	R		D	L
26 W I L L I A M S

Across
5. Act division
6. He hates his job and wants adventure
8. Amanda, Tom and Laura together
10. 'All pretty girls are a ____, a pretty ____'
11. Place where plays are performed
14. Jim called Laura Blue ____ by mistake
17. Jim asks Laura to do this
18. Play division
20. Laura was too sick to eat it
21. Laura quit business ____
22. ____ Menagerie
24. Amanda to Laura and Tom
25. Symbol for Laura
26. Author of The Glass Menagerie

Down
1. Place Laura liked to go instead of school
2. The gentleman caller
3. Amanda hopes for ____ callers for Laura
4. Glass____
5. Things that represent other things or have double meanings
6. Laura became physically ill during her first speed ____
7. Adjective to describe Amanda
8. Laura slipped on the ____ escape
9. Tom thinks causes of human action come from this
12. Mother of Tom and Laura
13. Setting of the play
15. Tom has paid his dues to the Merchant ____'s Union
16. Tom to Amanda
17. Laura to Amanda
19. Amanda wants to ____ Tom
23. She can't deal with the outside world
24. Amanda thinks causes of human action come from this

Glass Menagerie Crossword 4

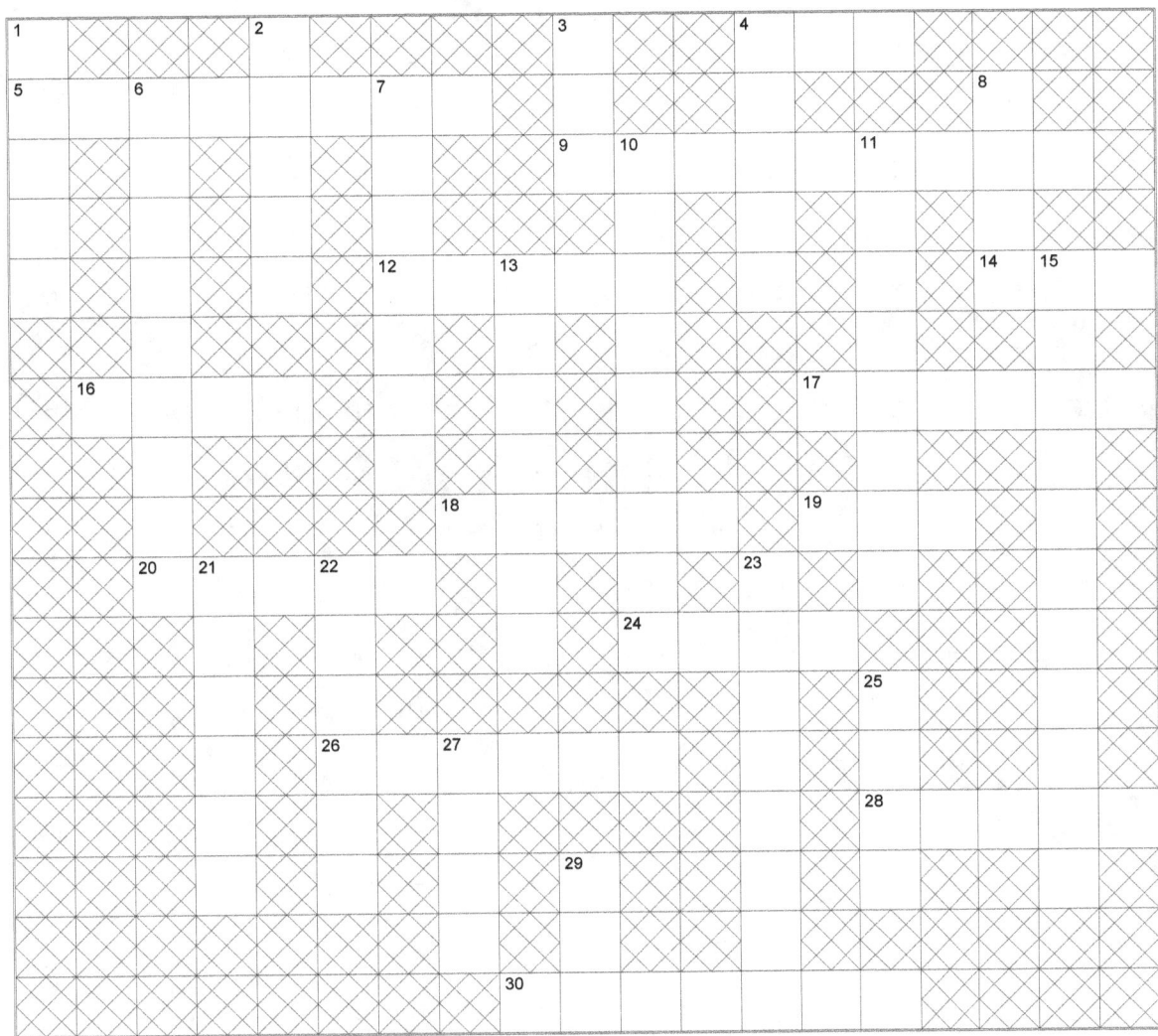

Across
4. Tom to Amanda
5. Author of Tom's novel Amanda returned to the library
9. Amanda sold these to make extra money
12. She can't deal with the outside world
14. He hates his job and wants adventure
16. Laura slipped on the ____ escape
17. Laura was too sick to eat it
18. Jim called Laura Blue ____ by mistake
19. Play division
20. Jim asks Laura to do this
24. 'All pretty girls are a ____, a pretty ____'
26. Amanda, Tom and Laura together
28. Act division
30. Amanda wants to ____ Tom

Down
1. ____ Menagerie
2. Jim's fiancee
3. The gentleman caller
4. Place where plays are performed
6. Laura's last name
7. Laura quit business ____
8. Laura became physically ill during her first speed ____
10. Setting of the play
11. Tom thinks causes of human action come from this
13. Symbol for Laura
15. Adjective to describe Amanda
21. Mother of Tom and Laura
22. Tom feels as if he is in a nailed up one
23. Laura to Amanda
25. Jim gives Laura one to make her realize she is pretty and appealing
27. Amanda thinks causes of human action come from this
29. Place Laura liked to go instead of school

Glass Menagerie Crossword 4 Answer Key

Across
4. Tom to Amanda
5. Author of Tom's novel Amanda returned to the library
9. Amanda sold these to make extra money
12. She can't deal with the outside world
14. He hates his job and wants adventure
16. Laura slipped on the ____ escape
17. Laura was too sick to eat it
18. Jim called Laura Blue ____ by mistake
19. Play division
20. Jim asks Laura to do this
24. 'All pretty girls are a ____, a pretty ____'
26. Amanda, Tom and Laura together
28. Act division
30. Amanda wants to ____ Tom

Down
1. ____ Menagerie
2. Jim's fiancee
3. The gentleman caller
4. Place where plays are performed
6. Laura's last name
7. Laura quit business ____
8. Laura became physically ill during her first speed ____
10. Setting of the play
11. Tom thinks causes of human action come from this
13. Symbol for Laura
15. Adjective to describe Amanda
21. Mother of Tom and Laura
22. Tom feels as if he is in a nailed up one
23. Laura to Amanda
25. Jim gives Laura one to make her realize she is pretty and appealing
27. Amanda thinks causes of human action come from this
29. Place Laura liked to go instead of school

Glass Menagerie

MIND	DAUGHTER	FIRE	INSTINCT	MAGAZINES
FAMILY	OVERBEARING	SEAMAN	COLLEGE	TOM
SCENE	WINGFIELD	FREE SPACE	CONTROL	WILLIAMS
SON	COFFIN	GENTLEMAN	APARTMENT	TRAP
BETTY	KISS	TEST	JIM	MOTHER

Glass Menagerie

ACT	LAURA	MENAGERIE	DINNER	LAWRENCE
STAGE	GLASS	DANCE	ROSES	SYMBOLS
UNICORN	AMANDA	FREE SPACE	JIM	TEST
KISS	BETTY	TRAP	APARTMENT	GENTLEMAN
COFFIN	SON	WILLIAMS	CONTROL	ZOO

Glass Menagerie

MENAGERIE	COLLEGE	SYMBOLS	LAURA	DAUGHTER
GENTLEMAN	LAWRENCE	FIRE	SCENE	STAGE
AMANDA	SON	FREE SPACE	DANCE	MOTHER
WINGFIELD	INSTINCT	MAGAZINES	WILLIAMS	TRAP
APARTMENT	ACT	KISS	BETTY	JIM

Glass Menagerie

UNICORN	ZOO	DINNER	MIND	CONTROL
TOM	TEST	ROSES	OVERBEARING	COFFIN
FAMILY	SEAMAN	FREE SPACE	BETTY	KISS
ACT	APARTMENT	TRAP	WILLIAMS	MAGAZINES
INSTINCT	WINGFIELD	MOTHER	DANCE	GLASS

Glass Menagerie

KISS	ZOO	MIND	INSTINCT	WILLIAMS
TOM	GLASS	SYMBOLS	WINGFIELD	LAWRENCE
BETTY	GENTLEMAN	FREE SPACE	COFFIN	FIRE
DANCE	OVERBEARING	JIM	TRAP	STAGE
SEAMAN	AMANDA	APARTMENT	ACT	ROSES

Glass Menagerie

MAGAZINES	UNICORN	SCENE	TEST	FAMILY
LAURA	COLLEGE	DAUGHTER	DINNER	MOTHER
SON	CONTROL	FREE SPACE	ACT	APARTMENT
AMANDA	SEAMAN	STAGE	TRAP	JIM
OVERBEARING	DANCE	FIRE	COFFIN	MENAGERIE

Copyrighted

Glass Menagerie

ACT	WINGFIELD	TOM	ROSES	COFFIN
GLASS	KISS	DINNER	COLLEGE	WILLIAMS
CONTROL	AMANDA	FREE SPACE	SEAMAN	FAMILY
MOTHER	STAGE	SCENE	TEST	UNICORN
MAGAZINES	BETTY	OVERBEARING	ZOO	TRAP

Glass Menagerie

JIM	INSTINCT	DANCE	SYMBOLS	MENAGERIE
SON	LAURA	GENTLEMAN	APARTMENT	FIRE
DAUGHTER	LAWRENCE	FREE SPACE	ZOO	OVERBEARING
BETTY	MAGAZINES	UNICORN	TEST	SCENE
STAGE	MOTHER	FAMILY	SEAMAN	MIND

Glass Menagerie

ACT	OVERBEARING	WINGFIELD	SEAMAN	WILLIAMS
FAMILY	DINNER	CONTROL	SCENE	MAGAZINES
AMANDA	FIRE	FREE SPACE	TRAP	SON
SYMBOLS	DANCE	GENTLEMAN	JIM	STAGE
MOTHER	UNICORN	MIND	LAURA	INSTINCT

Glass Menagerie

APARTMENT	GLASS	MENAGERIE	DAUGHTER	KISS
COFFIN	ZOO	COLLEGE	TEST	ROSES
BETTY	LAWRENCE	FREE SPACE	LAURA	MIND
UNICORN	MOTHER	STAGE	JIM	GENTLEMAN
DANCE	SYMBOLS	SON	TRAP	TOM

Glass Menagerie

DINNER	LAWRENCE	UNICORN	GLASS	ZOO
SCENE	COFFIN	SYMBOLS	KISS	MAGAZINES
WILLIAMS	JIM	FREE SPACE	APARTMENT	SON
INSTINCT	AMANDA	TRAP	SEAMAN	ROSES
STAGE	WINGFIELD	COLLEGE	DAUGHTER	MENAGERIE

Glass Menagerie

FAMILY	LAURA	FIRE	CONTROL	TEST
MIND	MOTHER	OVERBEARING	DANCE	BETTY
ACT	TOM	FREE SPACE	DAUGHTER	COLLEGE
WINGFIELD	STAGE	ROSES	SEAMAN	TRAP
AMANDA	INSTINCT	SON	APARTMENT	GENTLEMAN

Glass Menagerie

ROSES	GENTLEMAN	SCENE	WILLIAMS	LAURA
KISS	BETTY	OVERBEARING	MOTHER	MENAGERIE
LAWRENCE	GLASS	FREE SPACE	COLLEGE	INSTINCT
WINGFIELD	FAMILY	CONTROL	AMANDA	TOM
MIND	JIM	ACT	UNICORN	DINNER

Glass Menagerie

FIRE	SYMBOLS	SON	TEST	MAGAZINES
COFFIN	ZOO	APARTMENT	SEAMAN	DAUGHTER
DANCE	STAGE	FREE SPACE	UNICORN	ACT
JIM	MIND	TOM	AMANDA	CONTROL
FAMILY	WINGFIELD	INSTINCT	COLLEGE	TRAP

Glass Menagerie

LAURA	WILLIAMS	DAUGHTER	MIND	TEST
TRAP	JIM	DANCE	BETTY	SYMBOLS
GLASS	UNICORN	FREE SPACE	CONTROL	OVERBEARING
KISS	APARTMENT	WINGFIELD	STAGE	SCENE
ACT	COFFIN	MOTHER	FIRE	ROSES

Glass Menagerie

LAWRENCE	MENAGERIE	AMANDA	INSTINCT	COLLEGE
TOM	GENTLEMAN	FAMILY	SEAMAN	SON
MAGAZINES	DINNER	FREE SPACE	FIRE	MOTHER
COFFIN	ACT	SCENE	STAGE	WINGFIELD
APARTMENT	KISS	OVERBEARING	CONTROL	ZOO

Glass Menagerie

SEAMAN	GENTLEMAN	MAGAZINES	WINGFIELD	SYMBOLS
APARTMENT	ROSES	AMANDA	UNICORN	MOTHER
INSTINCT	MENAGERIE	FREE SPACE	ZOO	COFFIN
SON	DAUGHTER	TRAP	WILLIAMS	STAGE
ACT	FIRE	BETTY	TOM	COLLEGE

Glass Menagerie

TEST	KISS	CONTROL	FAMILY	JIM
DANCE	SCENE	LAWRENCE	DINNER	OVERBEARING
LAURA	GLASS	FREE SPACE	TOM	BETTY
FIRE	ACT	STAGE	WILLIAMS	TRAP
DAUGHTER	SON	COFFIN	ZOO	MIND

Glass Menagerie

APARTMENT	MIND	MOTHER	WILLIAMS	GLASS
COFFIN	CONTROL	FAMILY	TOM	STAGE
ZOO	SYMBOLS	FREE SPACE	DAUGHTER	INSTINCT
ROSES	UNICORN	WINGFIELD	FIRE	OVERBEARING
MAGAZINES	GENTLEMAN	LAURA	ACT	SCENE

Glass Menagerie

LAWRENCE	AMANDA	BETTY	DINNER	SEAMAN
TRAP	JIM	DANCE	COLLEGE	MENAGERIE
KISS	SON	FREE SPACE	ACT	LAURA
GENTLEMAN	MAGAZINES	OVERBEARING	FIRE	WINGFIELD
UNICORN	ROSES	INSTINCT	DAUGHTER	TEST

Glass Menagerie

TOM	DANCE	MOTHER	SYMBOLS	STAGE
LAURA	FIRE	GLASS	DINNER	ACT
UNICORN	TEST	FREE SPACE	LAWRENCE	SCENE
MIND	KISS	APARTMENT	WILLIAMS	ZOO
COLLEGE	INSTINCT	SEAMAN	BETTY	ROSES

Glass Menagerie

MENAGERIE	SON	GENTLEMAN	TRAP	MAGAZINES
COFFIN	FAMILY	CONTROL	DAUGHTER	JIM
WINGFIELD	OVERBEARING	FREE SPACE	BETTY	SEAMAN
INSTINCT	COLLEGE	ZOO	WILLIAMS	APARTMENT
KISS	MIND	SCENE	LAWRENCE	AMANDA

Glass Menagerie

OVERBEARING	APARTMENT	TRAP	STAGE	COLLEGE
ZOO	ACT	MAGAZINES	LAURA	LAWRENCE
MENAGERIE	WINGFIELD	FREE SPACE	DINNER	DANCE
SYMBOLS	GENTLEMAN	COFFIN	GLASS	MIND
AMANDA	SCENE	CONTROL	TEST	FAMILY

Glass Menagerie

JIM	ROSES	UNICORN	INSTINCT	WILLIAMS
KISS	FIRE	DAUGHTER	TOM	SON
MOTHER	SEAMAN	FREE SPACE	TEST	CONTROL
SCENE	AMANDA	MIND	GLASS	COFFIN
GENTLEMAN	SYMBOLS	DANCE	DINNER	BETTY

Glass Menagerie

LAWRENCE	MIND	SEAMAN	STAGE	WILLIAMS
COLLEGE	TEST	ACT	JIM	FAMILY
WINGFIELD	MAGAZINES	FREE SPACE	SON	MOTHER
ZOO	KISS	UNICORN	DANCE	DAUGHTER
CONTROL	INSTINCT	SCENE	SYMBOLS	OVERBEARING

Glass Menagerie

BETTY	GLASS	APARTMENT	COFFIN	FIRE
ROSES	MENAGERIE	DINNER	LAURA	TOM
AMANDA	GENTLEMAN	FREE SPACE	SYMBOLS	SCENE
INSTINCT	CONTROL	DAUGHTER	DANCE	UNICORN
KISS	ZOO	MOTHER	SON	TRAP

Glass Menagerie

DAUGHTER	OVERBEARING	KISS	GLASS	COFFIN
BETTY	GENTLEMAN	WINGFIELD	AMANDA	JIM
DINNER	APARTMENT	FREE SPACE	INSTINCT	STAGE
ZOO	ACT	COLLEGE	DANCE	CONTROL
TOM	LAWRENCE	MOTHER	TEST	ROSES

Glass Menagerie

MAGAZINES	SEAMAN	SCENE	WILLIAMS	LAURA
TRAP	FAMILY	SYMBOLS	MENAGERIE	MIND
SON	UNICORN	FREE SPACE	TEST	MOTHER
LAWRENCE	TOM	CONTROL	DANCE	COLLEGE
ACT	ZOO	STAGE	INSTINCT	FIRE

Glass Menagerie

LAURA	AMANDA	MENAGERIE	MAGAZINES	LAWRENCE
SCENE	GLASS	STAGE	ROSES	SYMBOLS
FAMILY	OVERBEARING	FREE SPACE	SON	INSTINCT
TOM	CONTROL	DINNER	MOTHER	TEST
GENTLEMAN	KISS	ACT	FIRE	DANCE

Glass Menagerie

DAUGHTER	BETTY	WILLIAMS	TRAP	COFFIN
SEAMAN	COLLEGE	UNICORN	MIND	APARTMENT
JIM	WINGFIELD	FREE SPACE	FIRE	ACT
KISS	GENTLEMAN	TEST	MOTHER	DINNER
CONTROL	TOM	INSTINCT	SON	ZOO

Glass Menagerie

OVERBEARING	MOTHER	ZOO	WILLIAMS	DAUGHTER
JIM	MENAGERIE	AMANDA	SCENE	APARTMENT
ROSES	DINNER	FREE SPACE	SYMBOLS	INSTINCT
LAURA	MIND	UNICORN	GLASS	FIRE
SON	DANCE	WINGFIELD	SEAMAN	MAGAZINES

Glass Menagerie

TOM	FAMILY	STAGE	KISS	LAWRENCE
BETTY	CONTROL	COLLEGE	COFFIN	GENTLEMAN
TRAP	ACT	FREE SPACE	SEAMAN	WINGFIELD
DANCE	SON	FIRE	GLASS	UNICORN
MIND	LAURA	INSTINCT	SYMBOLS	TEST

Glass Menagerie Vocabulary Word List

No.	Word	Clue/Definition
1.	APTITUDE	Ability; talent
2.	ARCHETYPE	An original model after which other similar things are patterned; prototype
3.	BELEAGUERED	Harassed by; surrounded by
4.	CANDELABRUM	A large decorative candlestick with several branches
5.	CONFISCATED	Took
6.	COURTING	Behaving so as to invite or incur
7.	DECEPTION	A ruse; a trick
8.	DISPOSITION	One's usual mood; temperament
9.	ELOQUENT	Characterized by persuasive, powerful discourse
10.	EMISSARY	An agent sent on a mission to represent another
11.	EMULATE	To try to equal or excel through imitation
12.	IMMINENT	About to happen
13.	INTIMATED	Hinted; told privately or subtly
14.	MARTYRED	Appeared as on who endures great suffering
15.	MASTICATION	Chewing
16.	MATRICULATING	Enrolling
17.	MENAGERIE	A collection of wild animals on exhibition
18.	NEGLIGENCE	Failure to exercise reasonable care
19.	OMINOUS	Threatening
20.	PATRONAGE	Support
21.	PLEUROSIS	Illness usually occurring as a complication of pneumonia
22.	PREPOSTEROUS	Absurd
23.	PROPAGANDA	Persuasive material put out by the advocates of a cause
24.	QUERULOUS	Given to complaining; peevish
25.	REJUVENATED	Made young again
26.	SATIRICAL	Using irony, sarcasm, or caustic wit to attack or expose folly, vice or stupidity
27.	SLIGHTED	Made small in size, degree, or amount; lacking
28.	SPECTER	A haunting or disturbing image or prospect
29.	TYRANNY	Extreme harshness or severity; rigor
30.	VESTIGE	A visible trace of something that exists no more

Copyrighted

Glass Menagerie Vocabulary Fill In The Blanks 1

_____ 1. Using irony, sarcasm, or caustic wit to attack or expose folly, vice or stupidity

_____ 2. Characterized by persuasive, powerful discourse

_____ 3. A collection of wild animals on exhibition

_____ 4. An agent sent on a mission to represent another

_____ 5. Made young again

_____ 6. Enrolling

_____ 7. Made small in size, degree, or amount; lacking

_____ 8. Behaving so as to invite or incur

_____ 9. Absurd

_____ 10. A visible trace of something that exists no more

_____ 11. A large decorative candlestick with several branches

_____ 12. Given to complaining; peevish

_____ 13. Took

_____ 14. Persuasive material put out by the advocates of a cause

_____ 15. About to happen

_____ 16. To try to equal or excel through imitation

_____ 17. Harassed by; surrounded by

_____ 18. Support

_____ 19. Chewing

_____ 20. Ability; talent

Glass Menagerie Vocabulary Fill In The Blanks 1 Answer Key

SATIRICAL	1. Using irony, sarcasm, or caustic wit to attack or expose folly, vice or stupidity
ELOQUENT	2. Characterized by persuasive, powerful discourse
MENAGERIE	3. A collection of wild animals on exhibition
EMISSARY	4. An agent sent on a mission to represent another
REJUVENATED	5. Made young again
MATRICULATING	6. Enrolling
SLIGHTED	7. Made small in size, degree, or amount; lacking
COURTING	8. Behaving so as to invite or incur
PREPOSTEROUS	9. Absurd
VESTIGE	10. A visible trace of something that exists no more
CANDELABRUM	11. A large decorative candlestick with several branches
QUERULOUS	12. Given to complaining; peevish
CONFISCATED	13. Took
PROPAGANDA	14. Persuasive material put out by the advocates of a cause
IMMINENT	15. About to happen
EMULATE	16. To try to equal or excel through imitation
BELEAGUERED	17. Harassed by; surrounded by
PATRONAGE	18. Support
MASTICATION	19. Chewing
APTITUDE	20. Ability; talent

Glass Menagerie Vocabulary Fill In The Blanks 2

1. Harassed by; surrounded by
2. An agent sent on a mission to represent another
3. Threatening
4. Made small in size, degree, or amount; lacking
5. A large decorative candlestick with several branches
6. Absurd
7. Took
8. A ruse; a trick
9. Given to complaining; peevish
10. Ability; talent
11. Enrolling
12. Illness usually occurring as a complication of pneumonia
13. A collection of wild animals on exhibition
14. To try to equal or excel through imitation
15. Extreme harshness or severity; rigor
16. Hinted; told privately or subtly
17. Support
18. One's usual mood; temperament
19. Behaving so as to invite or incur
20. Made young again

Glass Menagerie Vocabulary Fill In The Blanks 2 Answer Key

BELEAGUERED	1. Harassed by; surrounded by
EMISSARY	2. An agent sent on a mission to represent another
OMINOUS	3. Threatening
SLIGHTED	4. Made small in size, degree, or amount; lacking
CANDELABRUM	5. A large decorative candlestick with several branches
PREPOSTEROUS	6. Absurd
CONFISCATED	7. Took
DECEPTION	8. A ruse; a trick
QUERULOUS	9. Given to complaining; peevish
APTITUDE	10. Ability; talent
MATRICULATING	11. Enrolling
PLEUROSIS	12. Illness usually occurring as a complication of pneumonia
MENAGERIE	13. A collection of wild animals on exhibition
EMULATE	14. To try to equal or excel through imitation
TYRANNY	15. Extreme harshness or severity; rigor
INTIMATED	16. Hinted; told privately or subtly
PATRONAGE	17. Support
DISPOSITION	18. One's usual mood; temperament
COURTING	19. Behaving so as to invite or incur
REJUVENATED	20. Made young again

Glass Menagerie Vocabulary Fill In The Blanks 3

_____
_____
_____
_____
_____
_____
_____
_____
_____
_____
_____
_____
_____
_____
_____
_____
_____
_____
_____
_____

1. Using irony, sarcasm, or caustic wit to attack or expose folly, vice or stupidity
2. Made small in size, degree, or amount; lacking
3. Threatening
4. To try to equal or excel through imitation
5. An original model after which other similar things are patterned; prototype
6. Support
7. An agent sent on a mission to represent another
8. Behaving so as to invite or incur
9. Extreme harshness or severity; rigor
10. Made young again
11. Took
12. A visible trace of something that exists no more
13. Absurd
14. Characterized by persuasive, powerful discourse
15. Harassed by; surrounded by
16. Enrolling
17. About to happen
18. One's usual mood; temperament
19. Persuasive material put out by the advocates of a cause
20. Chewing

Glass Menagerie Vocabulary Fill In The Blanks 3 Answer Key

SATIRICAL	1. Using irony, sarcasm, or caustic wit to attack or expose folly, vice or stupidity
SLIGHTED	2. Made small in size, degree, or amount; lacking
OMINOUS	3. Threatening
EMULATE	4. To try to equal or excel through imitation
ARCHETYPE	5. An original model after which other similar things are patterned; prototype
PATRONAGE	6. Support
EMISSARY	7. An agent sent on a mission to represent another
COURTING	8. Behaving so as to invite or incur
TYRANNY	9. Extreme harshness or severity; rigor
REJUVENATED	10. Made young again
CONFISCATED	11. Took
VESTIGE	12. A visible trace of something that exists no more
PREPOSTEROUS	13. Absurd
ELOQUENT	14. Characterized by persuasive, powerful discourse
BELEAGUERED	15. Harassed by; surrounded by
MATRICULATING	16. Enrolling
IMMINENT	17. About to happen
DISPOSITION	18. One's usual mood; temperament
PROPAGANDA	19. Persuasive material put out by the advocates of a cause
MASTICATION	20. Chewing

Glass Menagerie Vocabulary Fill In The Blanks 4

_____ 1. A visible trace of something that exists no more

_____ 2. A ruse; a trick

_____ 3. Chewing

_____ 4. Hinted; told privately or subtly

_____ 5. Made young again

_____ 6. Made small in size, degree, or amount; lacking

_____ 7. Appeared as on who endures great suffering

_____ 8. An agent sent on a mission to represent another

_____ 9. Failure to exercise reasonable care

_____ 10. A collection of wild animals on exhibition

_____ 11. Extreme harshness or severity; rigor

_____ 12. Took

_____ 13. Threatening

_____ 14. One's usual mood; temperament

_____ 15. About to happen

_____ 16. Given to complaining; peevish

_____ 17. An original model after which other similar things are patterned; prototype

_____ 18. Using irony, sarcasm, or caustic wit to attack or expose folly, vice or stupidity

19. Enrolling

_____ 20. Behaving so as to invite or incur

Glass Menagerie Vocabulary Fill In The Blanks 4 Answer Key

VESTIGE	1. A visible trace of something that exists no more
DECEPTION	2. A ruse; a trick
MASTICATION	3. Chewing
INTIMATED	4. Hinted; told privately or subtly
REJUVENATED	5. Made young again
SLIGHTED	6. Made small in size, degree, or amount; lacking
MARTYRED	7. Appeared as on who endures great suffering
EMISSARY	8. An agent sent on a mission to represent another
NEGLIGENCE	9. Failure to exercise reasonable care
MENAGERIE	10. A collection of wild animals on exhibition
TYRANNY	11. Extreme harshness or severity; rigor
CONFISCATED	12. Took
OMINOUS	13. Threatening
DISPOSITION	14. One's usual mood; temperament
IMMINENT	15. About to happen
QUERULOUS	16. Given to complaining; peevish
ARCHETYPE	17. An original model after which other similar things are patterned; prototype
SATIRICAL	18. Using irony, sarcasm, or caustic wit to attack or expose folly, vice or stupidity
MATRICULATING	19. Enrolling
COURTING	20. Behaving so as to invite or incur

Glass Menagerie Vocabulary Matching 1

___ 1. IMMINENT
___ 2. MARTYRED
___ 3. MATRICULATING
___ 4. ELOQUENT
___ 5. PREPOSTEROUS
___ 6. OMINOUS
___ 7. PATRONAGE
___ 8. COURTING
___ 9. INTIMATED
___ 10. TYRANNY
___ 11. NEGLIGENCE
___ 12. QUERULOUS
___ 13. MASTICATION
___ 14. DECEPTION
___ 15. ARCHETYPE
___ 16. SLIGHTED
___ 17. CANDELABRUM
___ 18. EMISSARY
___ 19. CONFISCATED
___ 20. APTITUDE
___ 21. PROPAGANDA
___ 22. DISPOSITION
___ 23. MENAGERIE
___ 24. SATIRICAL
___ 25. REJUVENATED

A. Persuasive material put out by the advocates of a cause
B. Made small in size, degree, or amount; lacking
C. Extreme harshness or severity; rigor
D. Appeared as on who endures great suffering
E. Threatening
F. One's usual mood; temperament
G. A collection of wild animals on exhibition
H. Hinted; told privately or subtly
I. Using irony, sarcasm, or caustic wit to attack or expose folly, vice or stupidity
J. Given to complaining; peevish
K. Took
L. An original model after which other similar things are patterned; prototype
M. Chewing
N. Failure to exercise reasonable care
O. A large decorative candlestick with several branches
P. An agent sent on a mission to represent another
Q. Support
R. Enrolling
S. About to happen
T. Absurd
U. Behaving so as to invite or incur
V. A ruse; a trick
W. Characterized by persuasive, powerful discourse
X. Made young again
Y. Ability; talent

Glass Menagerie Vocabulary Matching 1 Answer Key

S - 1. IMMINENT
D - 2. MARTYRED
R - 3. MATRICULATING
W - 4. ELOQUENT
T - 5. PREPOSTEROUS
E - 6. OMINOUS
Q - 7. PATRONAGE
U - 8. COURTING
H - 9. INTIMATED
C - 10. TYRANNY
N - 11. NEGLIGENCE
J - 12. QUERULOUS
M - 13. MASTICATION
V - 14. DECEPTION
L - 15. ARCHETYPE
B - 16. SLIGHTED
O - 17. CANDELABRUM
P - 18. EMISSARY
K - 19. CONFISCATED
Y - 20. APTITUDE
A - 21. PROPAGANDA
F - 22. DISPOSITION
G - 23. MENAGERIE
I - 24. SATIRICAL
X - 25. REJUVENATED

A. Persuasive material put out by the advocates of a cause
B. Made small in size, degree, or amount; lacking
C. Extreme harshness or severity; rigor
D. Appeared as on who endures great suffering
E. Threatening
F. One's usual mood; temperament
G. A collection of wild animals on exhibition
H. Hinted; told privately or subtly
I. Using irony, sarcasm, or caustic wit to attack or expose folly, vice or stupidity
J. Given to complaining; peevish
K. Took
L. An original model after which other similar things are patterned; prototype
M. Chewing
N. Failure to exercise reasonable care
O. A large decorative candlestick with several branches
P. An agent sent on a mission to represent another
Q. Support
R. Enrolling
S. About to happen
T. Absurd
U. Behaving so as to invite or incur
V. A ruse; a trick
W. Characterized by persuasive, powerful discourse
X. Made young again
Y. Ability; talent

Glass Menagerie Vocabulary Matching 2

___ 1. INTIMATED
___ 2. CONFISCATED
___ 3. SLIGHTED
___ 4. COURTING
___ 5. DECEPTION
___ 6. MASTICATION
___ 7. MENAGERIE
___ 8. MATRICULATING
___ 9. OMINOUS
___10. SPECTER
___11. EMULATE
___12. PATRONAGE
___13. PLEUROSIS
___14. VESTIGE
___15. TYRANNY
___16. ARCHETYPE
___17. MARTYRED
___18. CANDELABRUM
___19. NEGLIGENCE
___20. ELOQUENT
___21. SATIRICAL
___22. QUERULOUS
___23. PROPAGANDA
___24. APTITUDE
___25. PREPOSTEROUS

A. A ruse; a trick
B. Extreme harshness or severity; rigor
C. Absurd
D. An original model after which other similar things are patterned; prototype
E. Threatening
F. Appeared as on who endures great suffering
G. Chewing
H. Support
I. Made small in size, degree, or amount; lacking
J. To try to equal or excel through imitation
K. Ability; talent
L. Persuasive material put out by the advocates of a cause
M. Using irony, sarcasm, or caustic wit to attack or expose folly, vice or stupidity
N. Hinted; told privately or subtly
O. Illness usually occurring as a complication of pneumonia
P. Behaving so as to invite or incur
Q. Characterized by persuasive, powerful discourse
R. A collection of wild animals on exhibition
S. A visible trace of something that exists no more
T. Failure to exercise reasonable care
U. Took
V. Enrolling
W. A haunting or disturbing image or prospect
X. Given to complaining; peevish
Y. A large decorative candlestick with several branches

Glass Menagerie Vocabulary Matching 2 Answer Key

N - 1. INTIMATED	A.	A ruse; a trick
U - 2. CONFISCATED	B.	Extreme harshness or severity; rigor
I - 3. SLIGHTED	C.	Absurd
P - 4. COURTING	D.	An original model after which other similar things are patterned; prototype
A - 5. DECEPTION	E.	Threatening
G - 6. MASTICATION	F.	Appeared as on who endures great suffering
R - 7. MENAGERIE	G.	Chewing
V - 8. MATRICULATING	H.	Support
E - 9. OMINOUS	I.	Made small in size, degree, or amount; lacking
W - 10. SPECTER	J.	To try to equal or excel through imitation
J - 11. EMULATE	K.	Ability; talent
H - 12. PATRONAGE	L.	Persuasive material put out by the advocates of a cause
O - 13. PLEUROSIS	M.	Using irony, sarcasm, or caustic wit to attack or expose folly, vice or stupidity
S - 14. VESTIGE	N.	Hinted; told privately or subtly
B - 15. TYRANNY	O.	Illness usually occurring as a complication of pneumonia
D - 16. ARCHETYPE	P.	Behaving so as to invite or incur
F - 17. MARTYRED	Q.	Characterized by persuasive, powerful discourse
Y - 18. CANDELABRUM	R.	A collection of wild animals on exhibition
T - 19. NEGLIGENCE	S.	A visible trace of something that exists no more
Q - 20. ELOQUENT	T.	Failure to exercise reasonable care
M - 21. SATIRICAL	U.	Took
X - 22. QUERULOUS	V.	Enrolling
L - 23. PROPAGANDA	W.	A haunting or disturbing image or prospect
K - 24. APTITUDE	X.	Given to complaining; peevish
C - 25. PREPOSTEROUS	Y.	A large decorative candlestick with several branches

Glass Menagerie Vocabulary Matching 3

___ 1. NEGLIGENCE	A. Enrolling
___ 2. EMULATE	B. A visible trace of something that exists no more
___ 3. CONFISCATED	C. Illness usually occurring as a complication of pneumonia
___ 4. SATIRICAL	D. Given to complaining; peevish
___ 5. PREPOSTEROUS	E. Support
___ 6. ARCHETYPE	F. Made small in size, degree, or amount; lacking
___ 7. REJUVENATED	G. Harassed by; surrounded by
___ 8. COURTING	H. Made young again
___ 9. SPECTER	I. Took
___10. MATRICULATING	J. About to happen
___11. IMMINENT	K. Persuasive material put out by the advocates of a cause
___12. PROPAGANDA	L. Failure to exercise reasonable care
___13. APTITUDE	M. An original model after which other similar things are patterned; prototype
___14. MASTICATION	N. Ability; talent
___15. MARTYRED	O. Hinted; told privately or subtly
___16. ELOQUENT	P. Appeared as on who endures great suffering
___17. INTIMATED	Q. A haunting or disturbing image or prospect
___18. QUERULOUS	R. Threatening
___19. PATRONAGE	S. Characterized by persuasive, powerful discourse
___20. SLIGHTED	T. One's usual mood; temperament
___21. OMINOUS	U. Absurd
___22. VESTIGE	V. Using irony, sarcasm, or caustic wit to attack or expose folly, vice or stupidity
___23. PLEUROSIS	W. To try to equal or excel through imitation
___24. BELEAGUERED	X. Behaving so as to invite or incur
___25. DISPOSITION	Y. Chewing

Glass Menagerie Vocabulary Matching 3 Answer Key

L - 1. NEGLIGENCE
W - 2. EMULATE
I - 3. CONFISCATED
V - 4. SATIRICAL
U - 5. PREPOSTEROUS
M - 6. ARCHETYPE
H - 7. REJUVENATED
X - 8. COURTING
Q - 9. SPECTER
A - 10. MATRICULATING
J - 11. IMMINENT
K - 12. PROPAGANDA
N - 13. APTITUDE
Y - 14. MASTICATION
P - 15. MARTYRED
S - 16. ELOQUENT
O - 17. INTIMATED
D - 18. QUERULOUS
E - 19. PATRONAGE
F - 20. SLIGHTED
R - 21. OMINOUS
B - 22. VESTIGE
C - 23. PLEUROSIS
G - 24. BELEAGUERED
T - 25. DISPOSITION

A. Enrolling
B. A visible trace of something that exists no more
C. Illness usually occurring as a complication of pneumonia
D. Given to complaining; peevish
E. Support
F. Made small in size, degree, or amount; lacking
G. Harassed by; surrounded by
H. Made young again
I. Took
J. About to happen
K. Persuasive material put out by the advocates of a cause
L. Failure to exercise reasonable care
M. An original model after which other similar things are patterned; prototype
N. Ability; talent
O. Hinted; told privately or subtly
P. Appeared as on who endures great suffering
Q. A haunting or disturbing image or prospect
R. Threatening
S. Characterized by persuasive, powerful discourse
T. One's usual mood; temperament
U. Absurd
V. Using irony, sarcasm, or caustic wit to attack or expose folly, vice or stupidity
W. To try to equal or excel through imitation
X. Behaving so as to invite or incur
Y. Chewing

Glass Menagerie Vocabulary Matching 4

___ 1. TYRANNY
___ 2. NEGLIGENCE
___ 3. OMINOUS
___ 4. IMMINENT
___ 5. REJUVENATED
___ 6. QUERULOUS
___ 7. MENAGERIE
___ 8. BELEAGUERED
___ 9. PROPAGANDA
___10. CONFISCATED
___11. DECEPTION
___12. SATIRICAL
___13. APTITUDE
___14. PLEUROSIS
___15. EMULATE
___16. MASTICATION
___17. ARCHETYPE
___18. SLIGHTED
___19. PATRONAGE
___20. ELOQUENT
___21. INTIMATED
___22. CANDELABRUM
___23. SPECTER
___24. MATRICULATING
___25. MARTYRED

A. About to happen
B. Took
C. Extreme harshness or severity; rigor
D. Persuasive material put out by the advocates of a cause
E. Illness usually occurring as a complication of pneumonia
F. Characterized by persuasive, powerful discourse
G. Hinted; told privately or subtly
H. An original model after which other similar things are patterned; prototype
I. A haunting or disturbing image or prospect
J. Enrolling
K. A collection of wild animals on exhibition
L. A ruse; a trick
M. Threatening
N. Made small in size, degree, or amount; lacking
O. Support
P. Appeared as on who endures great suffering
Q. Made young again
R. Chewing
S. Using irony, sarcasm, or caustic wit to attack or expose folly, vice or stupidity
T. Given to complaining; peevish
U. Ability; talent
V. To try to equal or excel through imitation
W. A large decorative candlestick with several branches
X. Harassed by; surrounded by
Y. Failure to exercise reasonable care

Glass Menagerie Vocabulary Matching 4 Answer Key

C - 1. TYRANNY
Y - 2. NEGLIGENCE
M - 3. OMINOUS
A - 4. IMMINENT
Q - 5. REJUVENATED
T - 6. QUERULOUS
K - 7. MENAGERIE
X - 8. BELEAGUERED
D - 9. PROPAGANDA
B - 10. CONFISCATED
L - 11. DECEPTION
S - 12. SATIRICAL
U - 13. APTITUDE
E - 14. PLEUROSIS
V - 15. EMULATE
R - 16. MASTICATION
H - 17. ARCHETYPE
N - 18. SLIGHTED
O - 19. PATRONAGE
F - 20. ELOQUENT
G - 21. INTIMATED
W - 22. CANDELABRUM
I - 23. SPECTER
J - 24. MATRICULATING
P - 25. MARTYRED

A. About to happen
B. Took
C. Extreme harshness or severity; rigor
D. Persuasive material put out by the advocates of a cause
E. Illness usually occurring as a complication of pneumonia
F. Characterized by persuasive, powerful discourse
G. Hinted; told privately or subtly
H. An original model after which other similar things are patterned; prototype
I. A haunting or disturbing image or prospect
J. Enrolling
K. A collection of wild animals on exhibition
L. A ruse; a trick
M. Threatening
N. Made small in size, degree, or amount; lacking
O. Support
P. Appeared as on who endures great suffering
Q. Made young again
R. Chewing
S. Using irony, sarcasm, or caustic wit to attack or expose folly, vice or stupidity
T. Given to complaining; peevish
U. Ability; talent
V. To try to equal or excel through imitation
W. A large decorative candlestick with several branches
X. Harassed by; surrounded by
Y. Failure to exercise reasonable care

Glass Menagerie Vocabulary Magic Squares 1

Match the definition with the vocabulary word. Put your answers in the magic squares below. When your answers are correct, all columns and rows will add to the same number.

A. MENAGERIE
B. MATRICULATING
C. SLIGHTED
D. INTIMATED
E. REJUVENATED
F. PLEUROSIS
G. ARCHETYPE
H. COURTING
I. SPECTER
J. DISPOSITION
K. TYRANNY
L. BELEAGUERED
M. EMISSARY
N. PROPAGANDA
O. OMINOUS
P. APTITUDE

1. Threatening
2. One's usual mood; temperament
3. Behaving so as to invite or incur
4. A collection of wild animals on exhibition
5. Hinted; told privately or subtly
6. Made young again
7. Extreme harshness or severity; rigor
8. Persuasive material put out by the advocates of a cause
9. Illness usually occurring as a complication of pneumonia
10. Made small in size, degree, or amount; lacking
11. An agent sent on a mission to represent another
12. Harassed by; surrounded by
13. A haunting or disturbing image or prospect
14. Ability; talent
15. Enrolling
16. An original model after which other similar things are patterned; prototype

A=	B=	C=	D=
E=	F=	G=	H=
I=	J=	K=	L=
M=	N=	O=	P=

Glass Menagerie Vocabulary Magic Squares 1 Answer Key

Match the definition with the vocabulary word. Put your answers in the magic squares below. When your answers are correct, all columns and rows will add to the same number.

A. MENAGERIE
B. MATRICULATING
C. SLIGHTED
D. INTIMATED
E. REJUVENATED
F. PLEUROSIS
G. ARCHETYPE
H. COURTING
I. SPECTER
J. DISPOSITION
K. TYRANNY
L. BELEAGUERED
M. EMISSARY
N. PROPAGANDA
O. OMINOUS
P. APTITUDE

1. Threatening
2. One's usual mood; temperament
3. Behaving so as to invite or incur
4. A collection of wild animals on exhibition
5. Hinted; told privately or subtly
6. Made young again
7. Extreme harshness or severity; rigor
8. Persuasive material put out by the advocates of a cause
9. Illness usually occurring as a complication of pneumonia
10. Made small in size, degree, or amount; lacking
11. An agent sent on a mission to represent another
12. Harassed by; surrounded by
13. A haunting or disturbing image or prospect
14. Ability; talent
15. Enrolling
16. An original model after which other similar things are patterned; prototype

A=4	B=15	C=10	D=5
E=6	F=9	G=16	H=3
I=13	J=2	K=7	L=12
M=11	N=8	O=1	P=14

Glass Menagerie Vocabulary Magic Squares 2

Match the definition with the vocabulary word. Put your answers in the magic squares below. When your answers are correct, all columns and rows will add to the same number.

A. SATIRICAL
B. NEGLIGENCE
C. EMULATE
D. PREPOSTEROUS
E. CANDELABRUM
F. REJUVENATED
G. PLEUROSIS
H. MENAGERIE
I. OMINOUS
J. ARCHETYPE
K. DISPOSITION
L. MATRICULATING
M. APTITUDE
N. INTIMATED
O. SPECTER
P. SLIGHTED

1. Made young again
2. Threatening
3. A haunting or disturbing image or prospect
4. Absurd
5. Ability; talent
6. Failure to exercise reasonable care
7. A collection of wild animals on exhibition
8. One's usual mood; temperament
9. To try to equal or excel through imitation
10. Made small in size, degree, or amount; lacking
11. An original model after which other similar things are patterned; prototype
12. A large decorative candlestick with several branches
13. Enrolling
14. Illness usually occurring as a complication of pneumonia
15. Using irony, sarcasm, or caustic wit to attack or expose folly, vice or stupidity
16. Hinted; told privately or subtly

A=	B=	C=	D=
E=	F=	G=	H=
I=	J=	K=	L=
M=	N=	O=	P=

Glass Menagerie Vocabulary Magic Squares 2 Answer Key

Match the definition with the vocabulary word. Put your answers in the magic squares below. When your answers are correct, all columns and rows will add to the same number.

A. SATIRICAL
B. NEGLIGENCE
C. EMULATE
D. PREPOSTEROUS
E. CANDELABRUM
F. REJUVENATED
G. PLEUROSIS
H. MENAGERIE
I. OMINOUS
J. ARCHETYPE
K. DISPOSITION
L. MATRICULATING
M. APTITUDE
N. INTIMATED
O. SPECTER
P. SLIGHTED

1. Made young again
2. Threatening
3. A haunting or disturbing image or prospect
4. Absurd
5. Ability; talent
6. Failure to exercise reasonable care
7. A collection of wild animals on exhibition
8. One's usual mood; temperament
9. To try to equal or excel through imitation
10. Made small in size, degree, or amount; lacking
11. An original model after which other similar things are patterned; prototype
12. A large decorative candlestick with several branches
13. Enrolling
14. Illness usually occurring as a complication of pneumonia
15. Using irony, sarcasm, or caustic wit to attack or expose folly, vice or stupidity
16. Hinted; told privately or subtly

A=15	B=6	C=9	D=4
E=12	F=1	G=14	H=7
I=2	J=11	K=8	L=13
M=5	N=16	O=3	P=10

Glass Menagerie Vocabulary Magic Squares 3

Match the definition with the vocabulary word. Put your answers in the magic squares below. When your answers are correct, all columns and rows will add to the same number.

A. ARCHETYPE
B. DECEPTION
C. REJUVENATED
D. BELEAGUERED
E. NEGLIGENCE
F. OMINOUS
G. MENAGERIE
H. MARTYRED
I. SLIGHTED
J. CANDELABRUM
K. PREPOSTEROUS
L. PLEUROSIS
M. IMMINENT
N. VESTIGE
O. MATRICULATING
P. PROPAGANDA

1. Appeared as on who endures great suffering
2. About to happen
3. A ruse; a trick
4. Absurd
5. A large decorative candlestick with several branches
6. Made young again
7. Persuasive material put out by the advocates of a cause
8. Failure to exercise reasonable care
9. Enrolling
10. Threatening
11. Made small in size, degree, or amount; lacking
12. Harassed by; surrounded by
13. An original model after which other similar things are patterned; prototype
14. Illness usually occurring as a complication of pneumonia
15. A collection of wild animals on exhibition
16. A visible trace of something that exists no more

A=	B=	C=	D=
E=	F=	G=	H=
I=	J=	K=	L=
M=	N=	O=	P=

Glass Menagerie Vocabulary Magic Squares 3 Answer Key

Match the definition with the vocabulary word. Put your answers in the magic squares below. When your answers are correct, all columns and rows will add to the same number.

A. ARCHETYPE
B. DECEPTION
C. REJUVENATED
D. BELEAGUERED
E. NEGLIGENCE
F. OMINOUS
G. MENAGERIE
H. MARTYRED
I. SLIGHTED
J. CANDELABRUM
K. PREPOSTEROUS
L. PLEUROSIS
M. IMMINENT
N. VESTIGE
O. MATRICULATING
P. PROPAGANDA

1. Appeared as on who endures great suffering
2. About to happen
3. A ruse; a trick
4. Absurd
5. A large decorative candlestick with several branches
6. Made young again
7. Persuasive material put out by the advocates of a cause
8. Failure to exercise reasonable care
9. Enrolling
10. Threatening
11. Made small in size, degree, or amount; lacking
12. Harassed by; surrounded by
13. An original model after which other similar things are patterned; prototype
14. Illness usually occurring as a complication of pneumonia
15. A collection of wild animals on exhibition
16. A visible trace of something that exists no more

A=13	B=3	C=6	D=12
E=8	F=10	G=15	H=1
I=11	J=5	K=4	L=14
M=2	N=16	O=9	P=7

Glass Menagerie Vocabulary Magic Squares 4

Match the definition with the vocabulary word. Put your answers in the magic squares below. When your answers are correct, all columns and rows will add to the same number.

A. EMISSARY
B. OMINOUS
C. QUERULOUS
D. ELOQUENT
E. MATRICULATING
F. DISPOSITION
G. DECEPTION
H. CANDELABRUM
I. MASTICATION
J. APTITUDE
K. COURTING
L. REJUVENATED
M. SLIGHTED
N. PROPAGANDA
O. ARCHETYPE
P. MENAGERIE

1. An agent sent on a mission to represent another
2. Persuasive material put out by the advocates of a cause
3. Ability; talent
4. Enrolling
5. A ruse; a trick
6. Made young again
7. A collection of wild animals on exhibition
8. Given to complaining; peevish
9. An original model after which other similar things are patterned; prototype
10. Characterized by persuasive, powerful discourse
11. A large decorative candlestick with several branches
12. Behaving so as to invite or incur
13. Chewing
14. One's usual mood; temperament
15. Threatening
16. Made small in size, degree, or amount; lacking

A=	B=	C=	D=
E=	F=	G=	H=
I=	J=	K=	L=
M=	N=	O=	P=

Glass Menagerie Vocabulary Magic Squares 4 Answer Key

Match the definition with the vocabulary word. Put your answers in the magic squares below. When your answers are correct, all columns and rows will add to the same number.

A. EMISSARY
B. OMINOUS
C. QUERULOUS
D. ELOQUENT
E. MATRICULATING
F. DISPOSITION
G. DECEPTION
H. CANDELABRUM
I. MASTICATION
J. APTITUDE
K. COURTING
L. REJUVENATED
M. SLIGHTED
N. PROPAGANDA
O. ARCHETYPE
P. MENAGERIE

1. An agent sent on a mission to represent another
2. Persuasive material put out by the advocates of a cause
3. Ability; talent
4. Enrolling
5. A ruse; a trick
6. Made young again
7. A collection of wild animals on exhibition
8. Given to complaining; peevish
9. An original model after which other similar things are patterned; prototype
10. Characterized by persuasive, powerful discourse
11. A large decorative candlestick with several branches
12. Behaving so as to invite or incur
13. Chewing
14. One's usual mood; temperament
15. Threatening
16. Made small in size, degree, or amount; lacking

A=1	B=15	C=8	D=10
E=4	F=14	G=5	H=11
I=13	J=3	K=12	L=6
M=16	N=2	O=9	P=7

Glass Menagerie Vocabulary Word Search 1

Words are placed backwards, forward, diagonally, up and down. Clues listed below can help you find the words. Circle the hidden vocabulary words in the maze.

```
I N E G L I G E N C E G A N O R T A P W
M N S L B Q M W Z H D L O Q C S Z E D Q
E C T R G M W J J P U I Y G Q N G N I D
N A F I E S S L L H T H S W D I M N S X
A N P B M J J R Q P I P Y B T P A R P Z
G D R E I A L T E M T H T S K R S K O V
E E S L S M T C C M P L E C X O T S S G
R L G E S F E E M O A V Y Y G P I U I Z
I A D A A D D H D D N R L E W A C O T L
E B E G R R L S F C H F L S P G A R I G
Z R R U Y L A P W Q D O I I Q A T E O Q
S U Y E L K C V K K Q S M S F N I T N H
L M T R X F I N R U R D X O C D O S T L
I S R E T R R Q E F H Q Q R B A N O X L
G M A D K K I N F B P Q U U R J T P M R
H E M U L A T E R E J U V E N A T E D L
T G R I S Z A G C N P R T L R Y P R D Y
E Y F F N D S D M J P C V P R U V P P K
D A R C H E T Y P E E J N A M M L G K B
Y Y R H G H N V M P W J N G H P Y O N D
W W Q S Z R J T S M D N J J N W R Q U J
C O U R T I N G R J Y O M I N O U S Z S
```

A collection of wild animals on exhibition (9)
A haunting or disturbing image or prospect (7)
A large decorative candlestick with several branches (11)
A ruse; a trick (9)
A visible trace of something that exists no more (7)
Ability; talent (8)
About to happen (8)
Absurd (12)
An agent sent on a mission to represent another (8)
An original model after which other similar things are patterned; prototype (9)
Appeared as on who endures great suffering (8)
Behaving so as to invite or incur (8)
Characterized by persuasive, powerful discourse (8)
Chewing (11)

Extreme harshness or severity; rigor (7)
Failure to exercise reasonable care (10)
Given to complaining; peevish (9)
Harassed by; surrounded by (11)
Hinted; told privately or subtly (9)
Illness usually occurring as a complication of pneumonia (9)
Made small in size, degree, or amount; lacking (8)
Made young again (11)
One's usual mood; temperament (11)
Persuasive material put out by the advocates of a cause (10)
Support (9)
Threatening (7)
To try to equal or excel through imitation (7)
Took (11)
Using irony, sarcasm, or caustic wit to attack or expose folly, vice or stupidity (9)

Glass Menagerie Vocabulary Word Search 1 Answer Key

Words are placed backwards, forward, diagonally, up and down. Clues listed below can help you find the words. Circle the hidden vocabulary words in the maze.

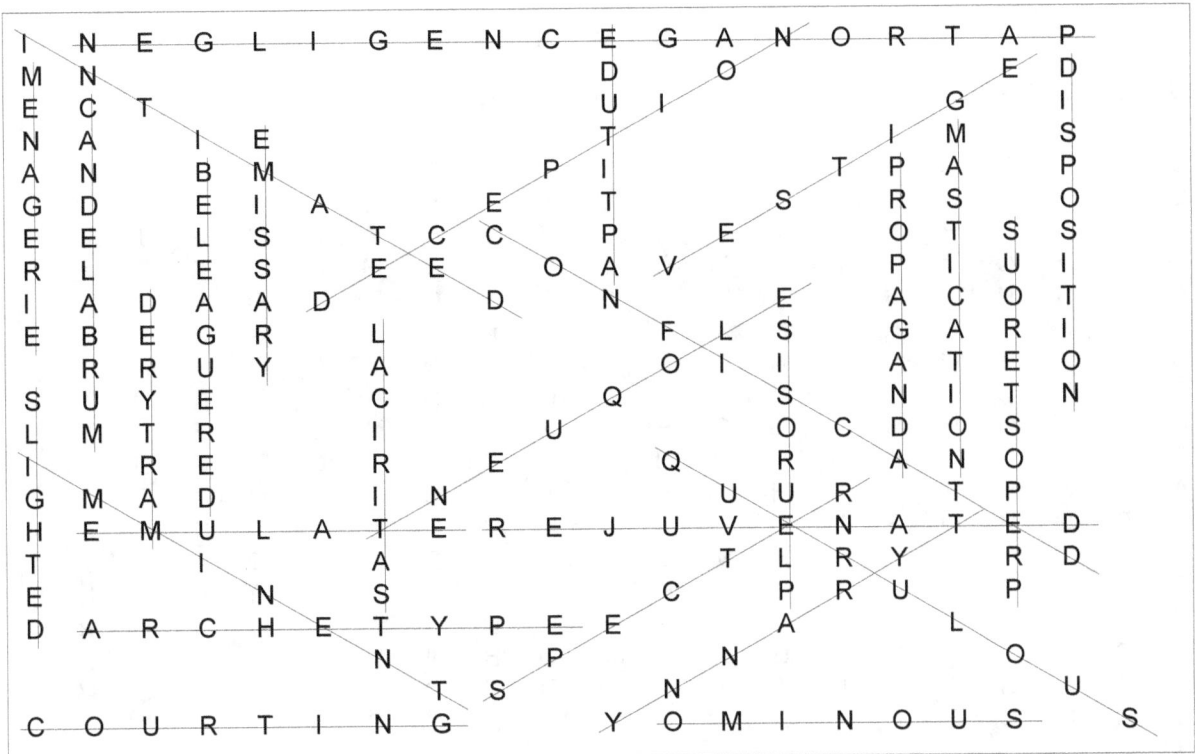

- A collection of wild animals on exhibition (9)
- A haunting or disturbing image or prospect (7)
- A large decorative candlestick with several branches (11)
- A ruse; a trick (9)
- A visible trace of something that exists no more (7)
- Ability; talent (8)
- About to happen (8)
- Absurd (12)
- An agent sent on a mission to represent another (8)
- An original model after which other similar things are patterned; prototype (9)
- Appeared as on who endures great suffering (8)
- Behaving so as to invite or incur (8)
- Characterized by persuasive, powerful discourse (8)
- Chewing (11)
- Extreme harshness or severity; rigor (7)
- Failure to exercise reasonable care (10)
- Given to complaining; peevish (9)
- Harassed by; surrounded by (11)
- Hinted; told privately or subtly (9)
- Illness usually occurring as a complication of pneumonia (9)
- Made small in size, degree, or amount; lacking (8)
- Made young again (11)
- One's usual mood; temperament (11)
- Persuasive material put out by the advocates of a cause (10)
- Support (9)
- Threatening (7)
- To try to equal or excel through imitation (7)
- Took (11)
- Using irony, sarcasm, or caustic wit to attack or expose folly, vice or stupidity (9)

Glass Menagerie Vocabulary Word Search 2

Words are placed backwards, forward, diagonally, up and down. Clues listed below can help you find the words. Circle the hidden vocabulary words in the maze.

```
D E C E P T I O N D V A C O U R T I N G
F S U O R E T S O P E R P S R G R O V S
S J M J C P Z N P Y G C H F B G I R F T
X X G W K L W L R X N H X G R T W G N K
S L I G H T E D B E Z E Z B I S G E B Q
Q F J K M U X T V C Q T Y S G N N R X Q
N H X M R B W Y B N S Y O H Y I C G J F
G N V O V J P R M E S P V B M C G X D X
M G S N D S R A V G S E H M D O Q F W N
A I H G R H O N X I A G I T E N A E X X
S Z X B Q R P N D L T D J N T F P I K V
T E P L J G A Y E G I E Z E A I T R D T
I X M N P S G G D E R R G U M S I E Q R
C K T I H K A G D N I Y X Q I C T G U N
A Q S R S N N H H P C T Z O T A U A E S
T G G P O S D O J S A R V L N T D N R X
I G M R E L A E M U L A T E I E E E U D
O K T B Z C B R G I H M V H S D Z M L L
N A R B G W T S Y G N U D C Z T H S O R
P C F Y T H D E J G J O B N S G I H U N
B E L E A G U E R E D D U D P G N G S M
C A N D E L A B R U M J B S G D Z T E B
```

A collection of wild animals on exhibition (9)
A haunting or disturbing image or prospect (7)
A large decorative candlestick with several branches (11)
A ruse; a trick (9)
A visible trace of something that exists no more (7)
Ability; talent (8)
About to happen (8)
Absurd (12)
An agent sent on a mission to represent another (8)
An original model after which other similar things are patterned; prototype (9)
Appeared as on who endures great suffering (8)
Behaving so as to invite or incur (8)
Characterized by persuasive, powerful discourse (8)
Chewing (11)

Extreme harshness or severity; rigor (7)
Failure to exercise reasonable care (10)
Given to complaining; peevish (9)
Harassed by; surrounded by (11)
Hinted; told privately or subtly (9)
Illness usually occurring as a complication of pneumonia (9)
Made small in size, degree, or amount; lacking (8)
Made young again (11)
One's usual mood; temperament (11)
Persuasive material put out by the advocates of a cause (10)
Support (9)
Threatening (7)
To try to equal or excel through imitation (7)
Took (11)
Using irony, sarcasm, or caustic wit to attack or expose folly, vice or stupidity (9)

Glass Menagerie Vocabulary Word Search 2 Answer Key

Words are placed backwards, forward, diagonally, up and down. Clues listed below can help you find the words. Circle the hidden vocabulary words in the maze.

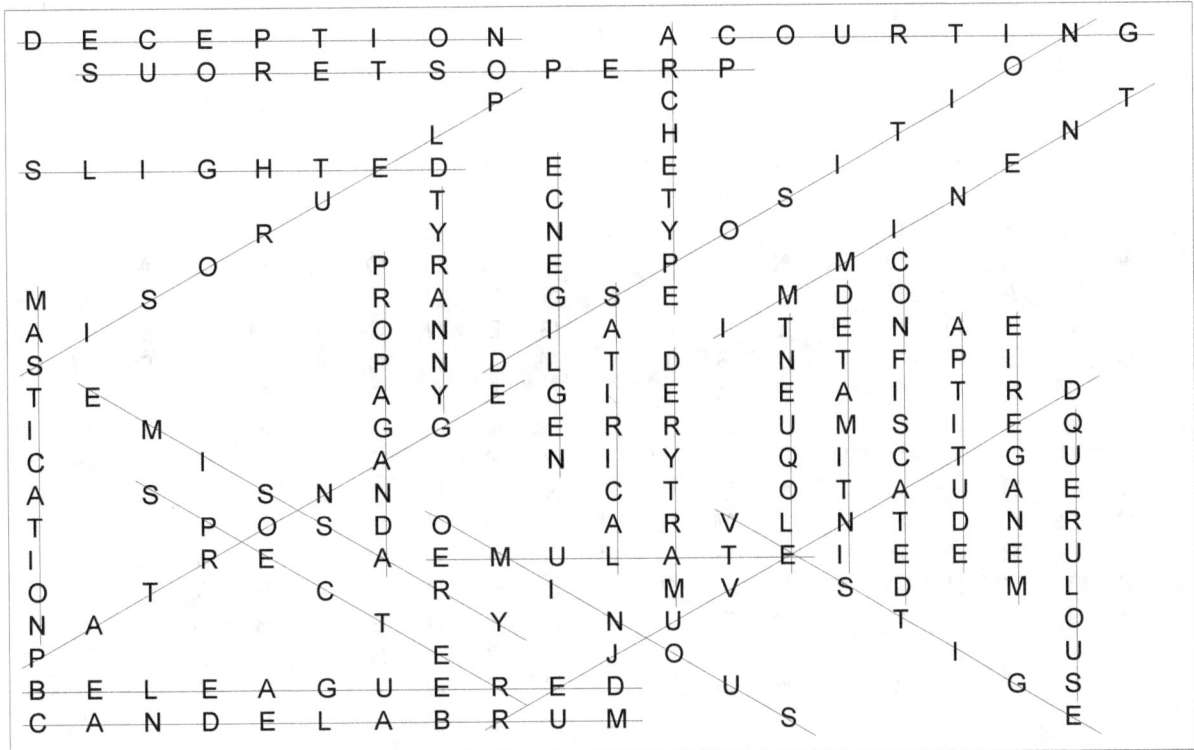

A collection of wild animals on exhibition (9)
A haunting or disturbing image or prospect (7)
A large decorative candlestick with several branches (11)
A ruse; a trick (9)
A visible trace of something that exists no more (7)
Ability; talent (8)
About to happen (8)
Absurd (12)
An agent sent on a mission to represent another (8)
An original model after which other similar things are patterned; prototype (9)
Appeared as on who endures great suffering (8)
Behaving so as to invite or incur (8)
Characterized by persuasive, powerful discourse (8)
Chewing (11)

Extreme harshness or severity; rigor (7)
Failure to exercise reasonable care (10)
Given to complaining; peevish (9)
Harassed by; surrounded by (11)
Hinted; told privately or subtly (9)
Illness usually occurring as a complication of pneumonia (9)
Made small in size, degree, or amount; lacking (8)
Made young again (11)
One's usual mood; temperament (11)
Persuasive material put out by the advocates of a cause (10)
Support (9)
Threatening (7)
To try to equal or excel through imitation (7)
Took (11)
Using irony, sarcasm, or caustic wit to attack or expose folly, vice or stupidity (9)

Glass Menagerie Vocabulary Word Search 3

Words are placed backwards, forward, diagonally, up and down. Words listed below are included in the maze. Circle the hidden vocabulary words in the maze.

```
T Y R A N N Y Q U E R U L O U S Y P C N
S R C R L N O I T A C I T S A M N S O W
L T A E M E P Y T E H C R A P E C D N H
Q P N J A O P C R C P O F H W N J F F T
J H D U R M Y M D N S U N K P A N N I L
P M E V T I B D V S A R V G Z G G O S V
A E L E Y N Q I T P T Z D T E T I C D
T M A N R O W N N L I I G Q Q R G T A S
R I B A E U L H Q T R N H J Z I N I T N
O S R T D S N E G L I G E N C E M S E X
N S U E E Q P J S T C M J K N K U O D W
A A M D C P S H A S A L A I D O E P E H
G R C J E F L L Z J L H M T R J M S R N
E Y B X P N U E I W J M P E E E U I E W
F P H S T C J M U G I X T L D L D U Y
Q C R C I K R L M R H S D V O U A W G B
K S T R O P E Z G H O T E J Q T T B A Y
N X T W N W T P X P P S E G U I E B E X
T A V K G C M E T T J I D E T B M L Y
M G T F F N E R L I B P C S N P B Z E S
P Y C T M Z P H G X X D C Q T A Z X B K
J K R L L N S E P R O P A G A N D A C V
```

APTITUDE	EMULATE	PLEUROSIS
ARCHETYPE	IMMINENT	PREPOSTEROUS
BELEAGUERED	INTIMATED	PROPAGANDA
CANDELABRUM	MARTYRED	QUERULOUS
CONFISCATED	MASTICATION	REJUVENATED
COURTING	MATRICULATING	SATIRICAL
DECEPTION	MENAGERIE	SLIGHTED
DISPOSITION	NEGLIGENCE	SPECTER
ELOQUENT	OMINOUS	TYRANNY
EMISSARY	PATRONAGE	VESTIGE

Glass Menagerie Vocabulary Word Search 3 Answer Key

Words are placed backwards, forward, diagonally, up and down. Words listed below are included in the maze. Circle the hidden vocabulary words in the maze.

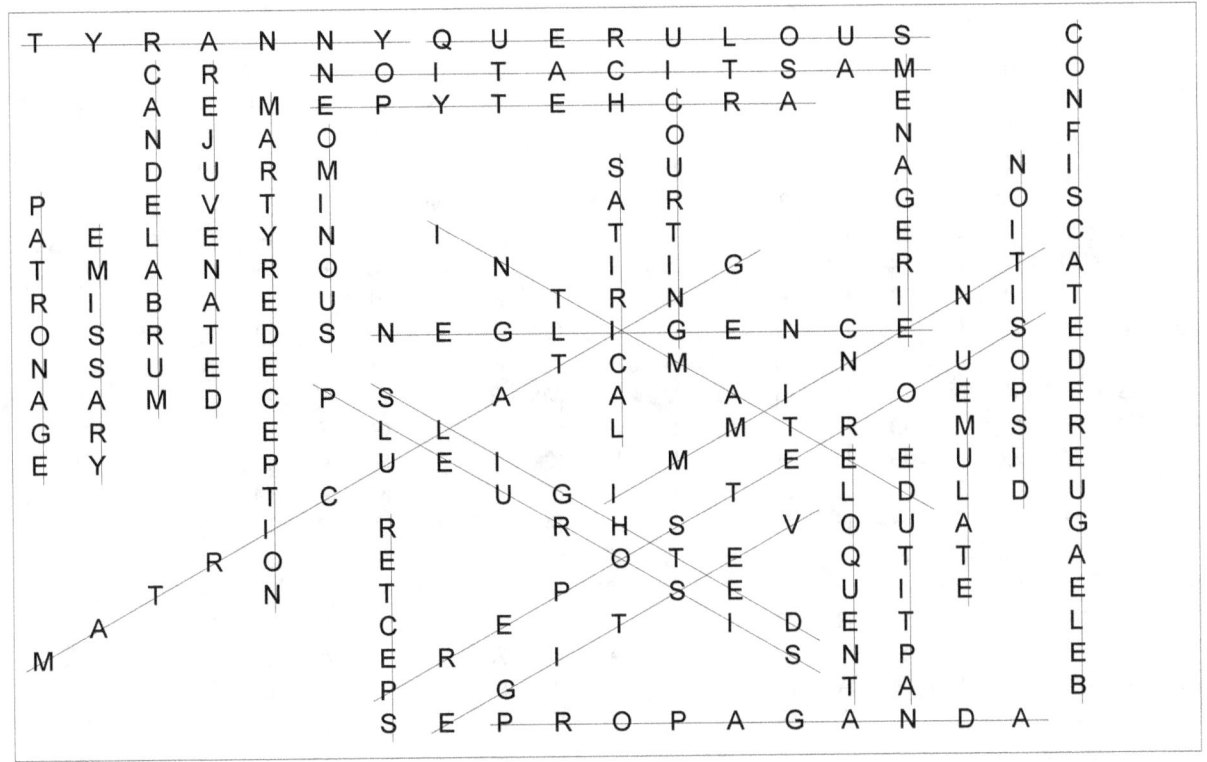

APTITUDE	EMULATE	PLEUROSIS
ARCHETYPE	IMMINENT	PREPOSTEROUS
BELEAGUERED	INTIMATED	PROPAGANDA
CANDELABRUM	MARTYRED	QUERULOUS
CONFISCATED	MASTICATION	REJUVENATED
COURTING	MATRICULATING	SATIRICAL
DECEPTION	MENAGERIE	SLIGHTED
DISPOSITION	NEGLIGENCE	SPECTER
ELOQUENT	OMINOUS	TYRANNY
EMISSARY	PATRONAGE	VESTIGE

Glass Menagerie Vocabulary Word Search 4

Words are placed backwards, forward, diagonally, up and down. Words listed below are included in the maze. Circle the hidden vocabulary words in the maze.

```
P M S L I G H T E D N D L X Y Z Q Q Y Y
R E H H G T W C R M O I X D D K W U T F
E N V Q G N N Y T R I S K E S N M E N W
P A K J M M Q N S K T P V T Z O U R N V
O G Z K I C Z N K R A O N A S I R E U D
S E L W N V J A V S C S Z M G T B L Q N
T R V T O S H R Y T I I H I L P A O O S
E I Q E U R A Y H B T T L T N E L U L V
R E C D S D E T A C S I F N O C E S E Z
O P V Z N T N D I M A O J I H E D C M W
U M K S N E I M W R M N F A D D N R U L
S G T V N L G Y V I M R Q X E A E L M
E Q S I S O R U E L P C S T G S C J A C
J M M Z H G L N W L H X A I F P X U T L
D M I C T V C D N E T L L L M E M V E Q
I N V S P H E D T J P G M J P C R E B X
V S Z Q S R V Y B B E C O U R T I N G T
L Z K S Y A P G X N W M B B S E T A Y C
L F P T K E R N Q G F G J M J R X T Q G
D M R N F S K Y R P A T R O N A G E N V
R A D N A G A P O R P A P T I T U D E R
M F B E L E A G U E R E D P Z D M N S R
```

APTITUDE
ARCHETYPE
BELEAGUERED
CANDELABRUM
CONFISCATED
COURTING
DECEPTION
DISPOSITION
ELOQUENT
EMISSARY

EMULATE
IMMINENT
INTIMATED
MARTYRED
MASTICATION
MENAGERIE
NEGLIGENCE
OMINOUS
PATRONAGE
PLEUROSIS

PREPOSTEROUS
PROPAGANDA
QUERULOUS
REJUVENATED
SATIRICAL
SLIGHTED
SPECTER
TYRANNY
VESTIGE

Glass Menagerie Vocabulary Word Search 4 Answer Key

Words are placed backwards, forward, diagonally, up and down. Words listed below are included in the maze. Circle the hidden vocabulary words in the maze.

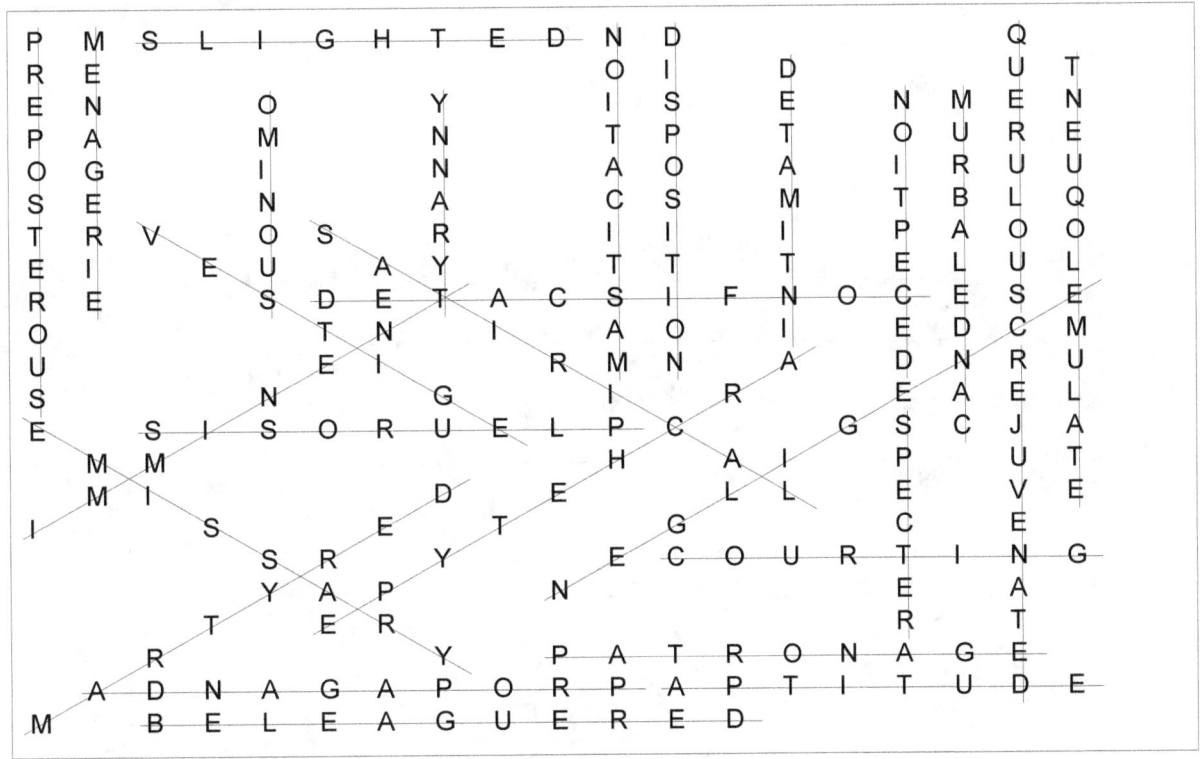

APTITUDE	EMULATE	PREPOSTEROUS
ARCHETYPE	IMMINENT	PROPAGANDA
BELEAGUERED	INTIMATED	QUERULOUS
CANDELABRUM	MARTYRED	REJUVENATED
CONFISCATED	MASTICATION	SATIRICAL
COURTING	MENAGERIE	SLIGHTED
DECEPTION	NEGLIGENCE	SPECTER
DISPOSITION	OMINOUS	TYRANNY
ELOQUENT	PATRONAGE	VESTIGE
EMISSARY	PLEUROSIS	

Glass Menagerie Vocabulary Crossword 1

Across
1. Failure to exercise reasonable care
4. Behaving so as to invite or incur
6. Made small in size, degree, or amount; lacking
7. A collection of wild animals on exhibition
8. Illness usually occurring as a complication of pneumonia
9. Ability; talent
14. About to happen
15. An original model after which other similar things are patterned; prototype
16. Appeared as on who endures great suffering

Down
2. A large decorative candlestick with several branches
3. Enrolling
4. Took
5. Extreme harshness or severity; rigor
6. A haunting or disturbing image or prospect
7. Chewing
8. Support
10. A ruse; a trick
11. Threatening
12. Hinted; told privately or subtly
13. An agent sent on a mission to represent another

Glass Menagerie Vocabulary Crossword 1 Answer Key

```
 1                   2
 N E G L I G E N C E                       3 M
                   A                         A
     4     5           6
     C O U R T I N G   S L I G H T E D
     O     Y   D       P         R
 7                   8
 M E N A G E R I E   P L E U R O S I S
 A   F     A   L     A   C         C
 S   I     N  9A P T I T U D E     U
 T   S     N   B   R   E   E       L
 I   C     Y   R   O   R   C       A
 C   A         U   N       E       T
 A   T    11O  M  12A      I   P   I
 T   E    M   13E   G      N   T   N
 I   D   14I M M I N E N T     I   G
 O       N     I           I   O
 N       O     S           M   N
         U     S           A
         S   15A R C H E T Y P E
                R              E
        16M A R T Y R E D      D
```

Across
1. Failure to exercise reasonable care
4. Behaving so as to invite or incur
6. Made small in size, degree, or amount; lacking
7. A collection of wild animals on exhibition
8. Illness usually occurring as a complication of pneumonia
9. Ability; talent
14. About to happen
15. An original model after which other similar things are patterned; prototype
16. Appeared as on who endures great suffering

Down
2. A large decorative candlestick with several branches
3. Enrolling
4. Took
5. Extreme harshness or severity; rigor
6. A haunting or disturbing image or prospect
7. Chewing
8. Support
10. A ruse; a trick
11. Threatening
12. Hinted; told privately or subtly
13. An agent sent on a mission to represent another

Glass Menagerie Vocabulary Crossword 2

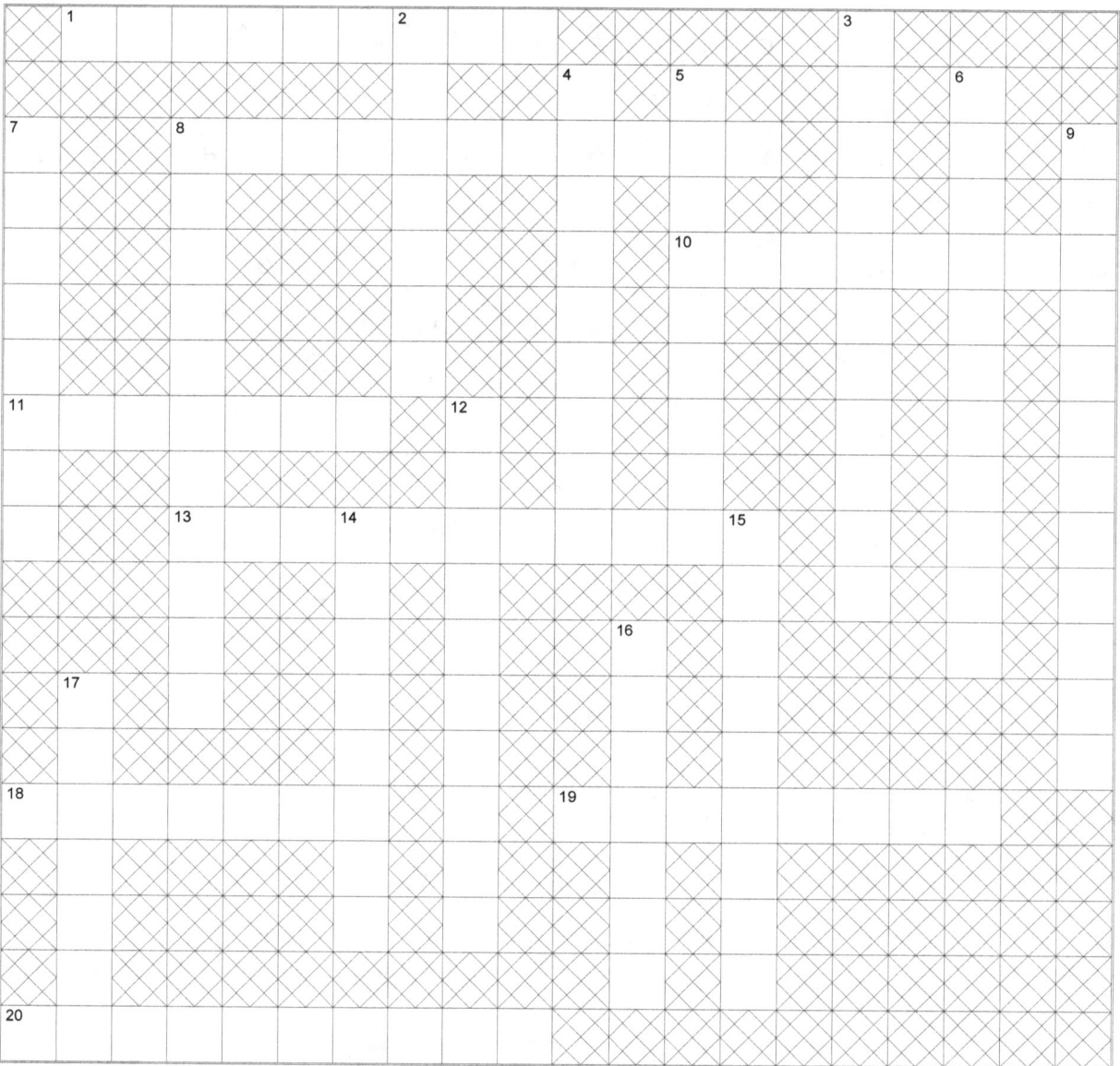

Across
1. Given to complaining; peevish
8. Took
10. Ability; talent
11. To try to equal or excel through imitation
13. Harassed by; surrounded by
18. A visible trace of something that exists no more
19. Appeared as on who endures great suffering
20. Persuasive material put out by the advocates of a cause

Down
2. Threatening
3. Chewing
4. Support
5. A collection of wild animals on exhibition
6. Made young again
7. About to happen
8. A large decorative candlestick with several branches
9. Absurd
12. Failure to exercise reasonable care
14. Characterized by persuasive, powerful discourse
15. A ruse; a trick
16. Extreme harshness or severity; rigor
17. A haunting or disturbing image or prospect

Glass Menagerie Vocabulary Crossword 2 Answer Key

	1 Q	U	E	R	U	2 L	O	U	S			3 M		
						O	M		4 P		5 M		A		6 R
7 I		8 C	O	N	F	I	S	C	A	T	E	D	S	E	9 P
M		A				N			T		N		T	J	R
M		N				O			R		10 A	P	T	I	T	U	D	E
I		D				U			O		G		C	V	P
N		E				S			N		E		A	E	O
11 E	M	U	L	A	T	E		12 N	A	G	R		T	N	S
N		A						E	G	I		I	A	T
T		13 B	E	L	14 E	A	G	U	E	R	15 E	D		O	T	E
		R			L				R	E	N	E	R
		U			L			16 T	C		D	O
		17 S	M		Q			Y	E			U
		P			U			R	P			S
18 V	E	S	T	I	G	E		19 M	A	R	T	Y	R	E	D
		C			N	C		A	I
		T			T	E		N	O
		E						Y	N
20 P	R	O	P	A	G	A	N	D	A

Across
1. Given to complaining; peevish
8. Took
10. Ability; talent
11. To try to equal or excel through imitation
13. Harassed by; surrounded by
18. A visible trace of something that exists no more
19. Appeared as on who endures great suffering
20. Persuasive material put out by the advocates of a cause

Down
2. Threatening
3. Chewing
4. Support
5. A collection of wild animals on exhibition
6. Made young again
7. About to happen
8. A large decorative candlestick with several branches
9. Absurd
12. Failure to exercise reasonable care
14. Characterized by persuasive, powerful discourse
15. A ruse; a trick
16. Extreme harshness or severity; rigor
17. A haunting or disturbing image or prospect

Glass Menagerie Vocabulary Crossword 3

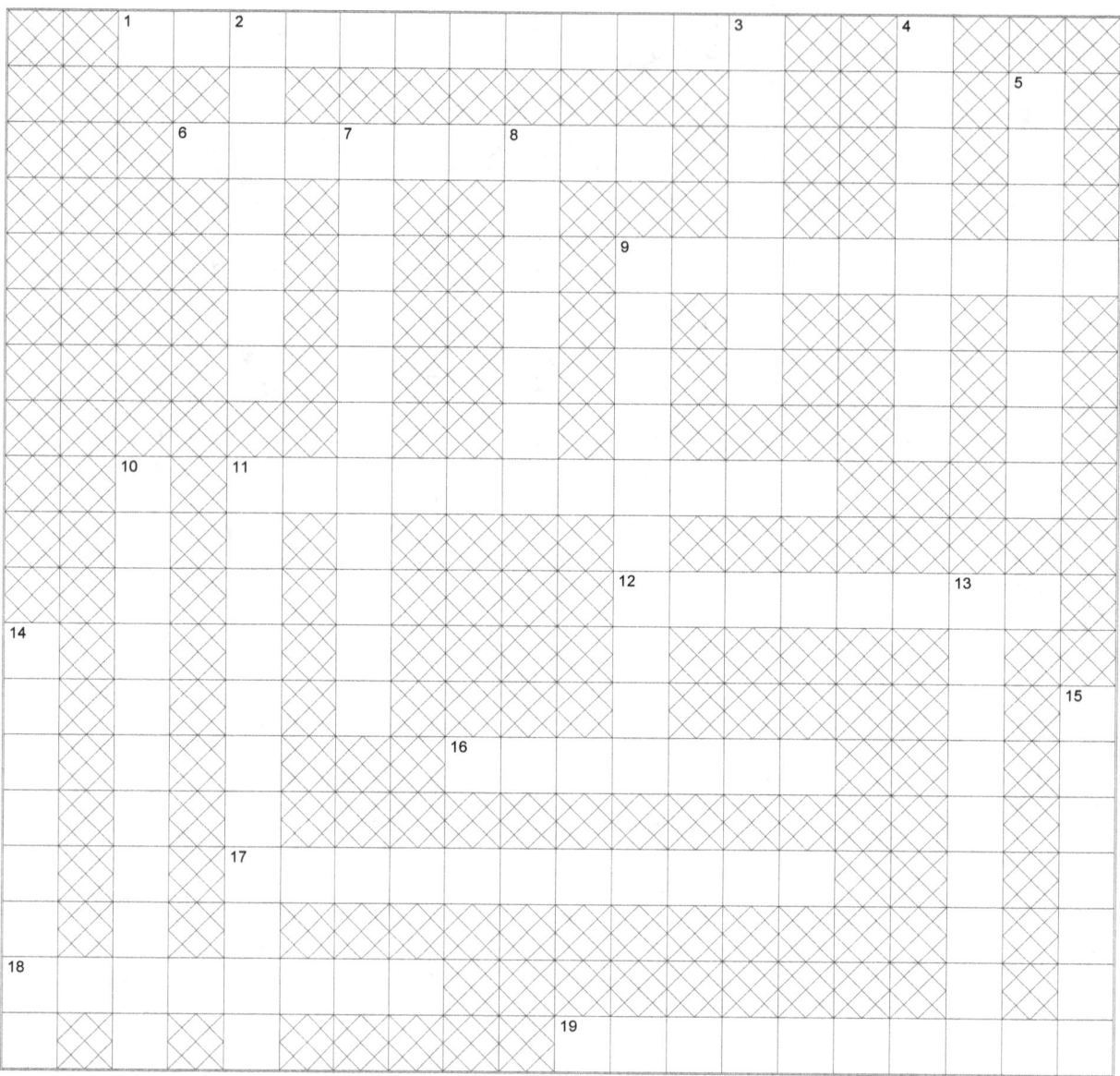

Across
1. Absurd
6. Given to complaining; peevish
9. Support
11. Took
12. Ability; talent
16. Extreme harshness or severity; rigor
17. Harassed by; surrounded by
18. Characterized by persuasive, powerful discourse
19. Failure to exercise reasonable care

Down
2. To try to equal or excel through imitation
3. A haunting or disturbing image or prospect
4. About to happen
5. Made small in size, degree, or amount; lacking
7. Made young again
8. Threatening
9. Persuasive material put out by the advocates of a cause
10. Chewing
11. A large decorative candlestick with several branches
13. A ruse; a trick
14. Appeared as on who endures great suffering
15. A visible trace of something that exists no more

Glass Menagerie Vocabulary Crossword 3 Answer Key

	1 P	2 E	P	O	S	T	E	R	O	3 U	S		4 I		
		M									P		M	5 S	
		6 Q	U	7 E	R	U	8 L	O	U	S			M	L	
			L		E		M				C		I	I	
			A		J		I		9 P	A	T	R	O	N	A	G	E
			T		U		N		R		E		E	H	
			E		V		O		O		R		N	T	
					E		U		P				T	E	
		10 M	11 C	O	N	F	I	S	C	A	T	E	D		
		A		A		A			A						
		S		N		T			12 A	P	T	I	T	13 U	D	E
14 M		T		D		E			N				E		
A		I		E		D			D				C		15 V
R		C		L				16 T	Y	R	A	N	N	Y	E
T		A		A									P		S
Y		T		17 B	E	L	E	A	G	U	E	R	E	D	T
R		I		R									I		I
18 E	L	O	Q	U	E	N	T						O		G
D		N		M				19 N	E	G	L	I	G	E	N	C	E

Across
1. Absurd
6. Given to complaining; peevish
9. Support
11. Took
12. Ability; talent
16. Extreme harshness or severity; rigor
17. Harassed by; surrounded by
18. Characterized by persuasive, powerful discourse
19. Failure to exercise reasonable care

Down
2. To try to equal or excel through imitation
3. A haunting or disturbing image or prospect
4. About to happen
5. Made small in size, degree, or amount; lacking
7. Made young again
8. Threatening
9. Persuasive material put out by the advocates of a cause
10. Chewing
11. A large decorative candlestick with several branches
13. A ruse; a trick
14. Appeared as on who endures great suffering
15. A visible trace of something that exists no more

Glass Menagerie Vocabulary Crossword 4

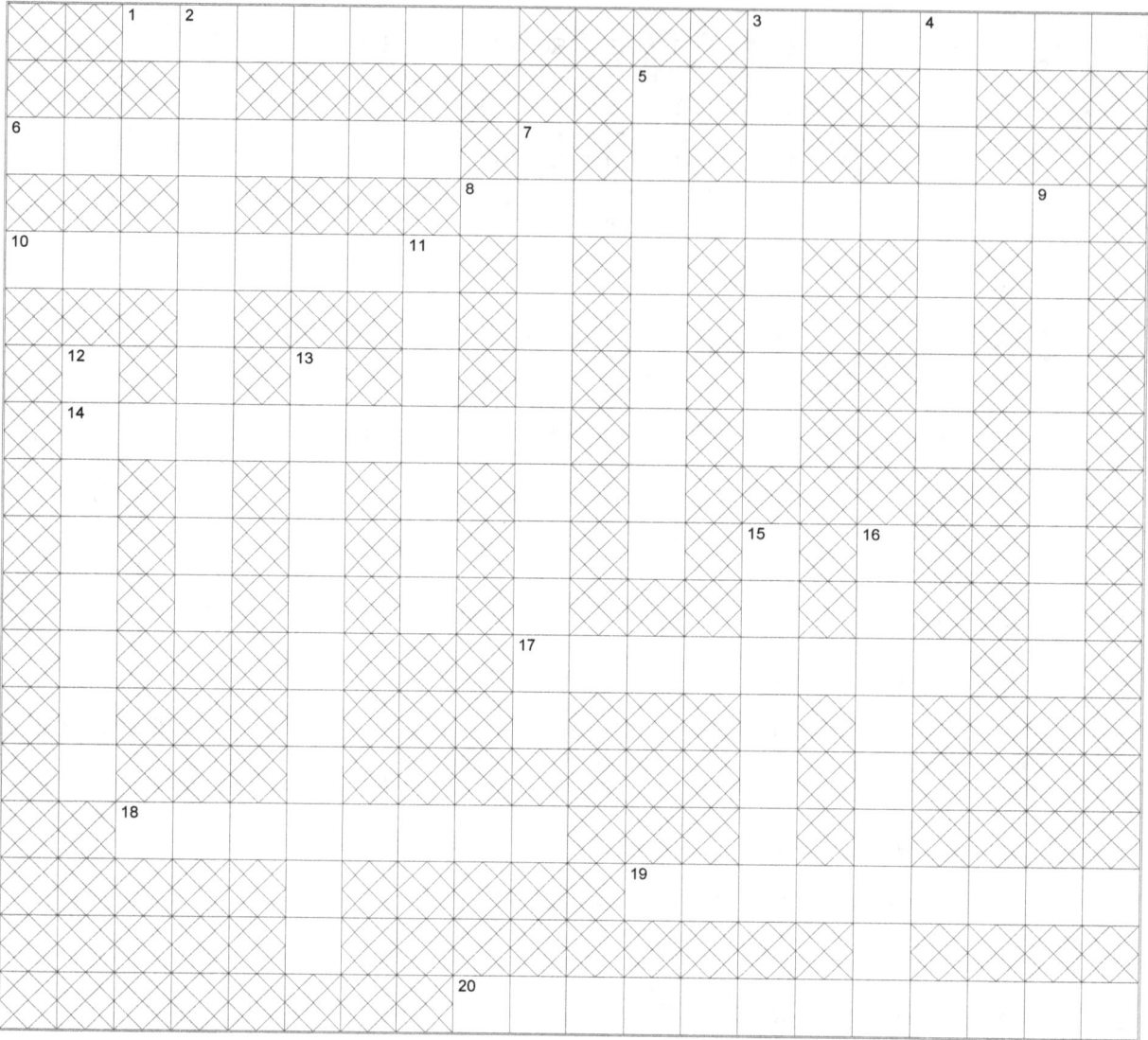

Across
1. Threatening
3. A haunting or disturbing image or prospect
6. An agent sent on a mission to represent another
8. Harassed by; surrounded by
10. About to happen
14. Support
17. Characterized by persuasive, powerful discourse
18. Appeared as on who endures great suffering
19. Illness usually occurring as a complication of pneumonia
20. Absurd

Down
2. Chewing
3. Made small in size, degree, or amount; lacking
4. Behaving so as to invite or incur
5. Given to complaining; peevish
7. Made young again
9. A ruse; a trick
11. Extreme harshness or severity; rigor
12. Ability; talent
13. Took
15. To try to equal or excel through imitation
16. A collection of wild animals on exhibition

Glass Menagerie Vocabulary Crossword 4 Answer Key

Across
1. Threatening
3. A haunting or disturbing image or prospect
6. An agent sent on a mission to represent another
8. Harassed by; surrounded by
10. About to happen
14. Support
17. Characterized by persuasive, powerful discourse
18. Appeared as on who endures great suffering
19. Illness usually occurring as a complication of pneumonia
20. Absurd

Down
2. Chewing
3. Made small in size, degree, or amount; lacking
4. Behaving so as to invite or incur
5. Given to complaining; peevish
7. Made young again
9. A ruse; a trick
11. Extreme harshness or severity; rigor
12. Ability; talent
13. Took
15. To try to equal or excel through imitation
16. A collection of wild animals on exhibition

Glass Menagerie Vocabulary Juggle Letters 1

1. NTMITACOASI = 1. _____
Chewing

2. UTMINIGCAATLR = 2. _____
Enrolling

3. GSVTIEE = 3. _____
A visible trace of something that exists no more

4. EAEINMRGE = 4. _____
A collection of wild animals on exhibition

5. NITTEIDAM = 5. _____
Hinted; told privately or subtly

6. ECREPYHAT = 6. _____
An original model after which other similar things are patterned; prototype

7. ITEIMMNN = 7. _____
About to happen

8. DRAULMNBCAE = 8. _____
A large decorative candlestick with several branches

9. ILETHSDG = 9. _____
Made small in size, degree, or amount; lacking

10. OAGANPETR =10. _____
Support

11. EDAEURELEGB =11. _____
Harassed by; surrounded by

12. DPGRPAANAO =12. _____
Persuasive material put out by the advocates of a cause

13. ARIITLACS =13. _____
Using irony, sarcasm, or caustic wit to attack or expose folly, vice or stupidity

14. CSEEPRT =14. _____
A haunting or disturbing image or prospect

15. TDRREYAM =15. _____
Appeared as on who endures great suffering

Glass Menagerie Vocabulary Juggle Letters 1 Answer Key

1. NTMITACOASI = 1. MASTICATION
   Chewing

2. UTMINIGCAATLR = 2. MATRICULATING
   Enrolling

3. GSVTIEE = 3. VESTIGE
   A visible trace of something that exists no more

4. EAEINMRGE = 4. MENAGERIE
   A collection of wild animals on exhibition

5. NITTEIDAM = 5. INTIMATED
   Hinted; told privately or subtly

6. ECREPYHAT = 6. ARCHETYPE
   An original model after which other similar things are patterned; prototype

7. ITEIMMNN = 7. IMMINENT
   About to happen

8. DRAULMNBCAE = 8. CANDELABRUM
   A large decorative candlestick with several branches

9. ILETHSDG = 9. SLIGHTED
   Made small in size, degree, or amount; lacking

10. OAGANPETR =10. PATRONAGE
    Support

11. EDAEURELEGB =11. BELEAGUERED
    Harassed by; surrounded by

12. DPGRPAANAO =12. PROPAGANDA
    Persuasive material put out by the advocates of a cause

13. ARIITLACS =13. SATIRICAL
    Using irony, sarcasm, or caustic wit to attack or expose folly, vice or stupidity

14. CSEEPRT =14. SPECTER
    A haunting or disturbing image or prospect

15. TDRREYAM =15. MARTYRED
    Appeared as on who endures great suffering

Glass Menagerie Vocabulary Juggle Letters 2

1. ITCSIARLA = 1. _____
Using irony, sarcasm, or caustic wit to attack or expose folly, vice or stupidity

2. SROUEILSP = 2. _____
Illness usually occurring as a complication of pneumonia

3. OSULUREUQ = 3. _____
Given to complaining; peevish

4. PPOEUTROSRES = 4. _____
Absurd

5. EETSCRP = 5. _____
A haunting or disturbing image or prospect

6. RDEATMRY = 6. _____
Appeared as on who endures great suffering

7. EEDTNVJAERU = 7. _____
Made young again

8. EGRAUDEBELE = 8. _____
Harassed by; surrounded by

9. AETSNCOIFCD = 9. _____
Took

10. TPDOENIEC = 10. _____
A ruse; a trick

11. NAOAAGPPDR = 11. _____
Persuasive material put out by the advocates of a cause

12. EEGNNILCGE = 12. _____
Failure to exercise reasonable care

13. ATNIDMITE = 13. _____
Hinted; told privately or subtly

14. SIOODINSTIP = 14. _____
One's usual mood; temperament

15. OOSNMIU = 15. _____
Threatening

Glass Menagerie Vocabulary Juggle Letters 2 Answer Key

1. ITCSIARLA = 1. SATIRICAL
   Using irony, sarcasm, or caustic wit to attack or expose folly, vice or stupidity

2. SROUEILSP = 2. PLEUROSIS
   Illness usually occurring as a complication of pneumonia

3. OSULUREUQ = 3. QUERULOUS
   Given to complaining; peevish

4. PPOEUTROSRES = 4. PREPOSTEROUS
   Absurd

5. EETSCRP = 5. SPECTER
   A haunting or disturbing image or prospect

6. RDEATMRY = 6. MARTYRED
   Appeared as on who endures great suffering

7. EEDTNVJAERU = 7. REJUVENATED
   Made young again

8. EGRAUDEBELE = 8. BELEAGUERED
   Harassed by; surrounded by

9. AETSNCOIFCD = 9. CONFISCATED
   Took

10. TPDOENIEC = 10. DECEPTION
    A ruse; a trick

11. NAOAAGPPDR = 11. PROPAGANDA
    Persuasive material put out by the advocates of a cause

12. EEGNNILCGE = 12. NEGLIGENCE
    Failure to exercise reasonable care

13. ATNIDMITE = 13. INTIMATED
    Hinted; told privately or subtly

14. SIOODINSTIP = 14. DISPOSITION
    One's usual mood; temperament

15. OOSNMIU = 15. OMINOUS
    Threatening

Glass Menagerie Vocabulary Juggle Letters 3

1. EETIGVS = 1. _____
A visible trace of something that exists no more

2. LCGNNGIEEE = 2. _____
Failure to exercise reasonable care

3. IUCNGRTO = 3. _____
Behaving so as to invite or incur

4. EDOTIPENC = 4. _____
A ruse; a trick

5. ADAGPORAPN = 5. _____
Persuasive material put out by the advocates of a cause

6. EURUOLSQU = 6. _____
Given to complaining; peevish

7. CTAPEYEHR = 7. _____
An original model after which other similar things are patterned; prototype

8. EMTEAUL = 8. _____
To try to equal or excel through imitation

9. ARTLIACSI = 9. _____
Using irony, sarcasm, or caustic wit to attack or expose folly, vice or stupidity

10. VJEUDAENRTE = 10. _____
Made young again

11. NOAAGTPRE = 11. _____
Support

12. AALIGRTIUCMTN = 12. _____
Enrolling

13. UADIEPTT = 13. _____
Ability; talent

14. LOSUPISRE = 14. _____
Illness usually occurring as a complication of pneumonia

15. EENRMEAGI = 15. _____
A collection of wild animals on exhibition

Glass Menagerie Vocabulary Juggle Letters 3 Answer Key

1. EETIGVS = 1. VESTIGE
A visible trace of something that exists no more

2. LCGNNGIEEE = 2. NEGLIGENCE
Failure to exercise reasonable care

3. IUCNGRTO = 3. COURTING
Behaving so as to invite or incur

4. EDOTIPENC = 4. DECEPTION
A ruse; a trick

5. ADAGPORAPN = 5. PROPAGANDA
Persuasive material put out by the advocates of a cause

6. EURUOLSQU = 6. QUERULOUS
Given to complaining; peevish

7. CTAPEYEHR = 7. ARCHETYPE
An original model after which other similar things are patterned; prototype

8. EMTEAUL = 8. EMULATE
To try to equal or excel through imitation

9. ARTLIACSI = 9. SATIRICAL
Using irony, sarcasm, or caustic wit to attack or expose folly, vice or stupidity

10. VJEUDAENRTE =10. REJUVENATED
Made young again

11. NOAAGTPRE =11. PATRONAGE
Support

12. AALIGRTIUCMTN =12. MATRICULATING
Enrolling

13. UADIEPTT =13. APTITUDE
Ability; talent

14. LOSUPISRE =14. PLEUROSIS
Illness usually occurring as a complication of pneumonia

15. EENRMEAGI =15. MENAGERIE
A collection of wild animals on exhibition

Glass Menagerie Vocabulary Juggle Letters 4

1. LUEUROUQS = 1. _____
Given to complaining; peevish

2. ERPSOSRTUPOE = 2. _____
Absurd

3. AASCTMOTNII = 3. _____
Chewing

4. ELEUNQTO = 4. _____
Characterized by persuasive, powerful discourse

5. DAUTEPIT = 5. _____
Ability; talent

6. IEDTHLGS = 6. _____
Made small in size, degree, or amount; lacking

7. GABEDUELEER = 7. _____
Harassed by; surrounded by

8. ERMANGEEI = 8. _____
A collection of wild animals on exhibition

9. EDNARVTEEUJ = 9. _____
Made young again

10. CTRESEP = 10. _____
A haunting or disturbing image or prospect

11. MSONIOU = 11. _____
Threatening

12. AOANDAPPRG = 12. _____
Persuasive material put out by the advocates of a cause

13. AENTGPARO = 13. _____
Support

14. UEMATLE = 14. _____
To try to equal or excel through imitation

15. PETDCONEI = 15. _____
A ruse; a trick

Glass Menagerie Vocabulary Juggle Letters 4 Answer Key

1. LUEUROUQS = 1. QUERULOUS
Given to complaining; peevish

2. ERPSOSRTUPOE = 2. PREPOSTEROUS
Absurd

3. AASCTMOTNII = 3. MASTICATION
Chewing

4. ELEUNQTO = 4. ELOQUENT
Characterized by persuasive, powerful discourse

5. DAUTEPIT = 5. APTITUDE
Ability; talent

6. IEDTHLGS = 6. SLIGHTED
Made small in size, degree, or amount; lacking

7. GABEDUELEER = 7. BELEAGUERED
Harassed by; surrounded by

8. ERMANGEEI = 8. MENAGERIE
A collection of wild animals on exhibition

9. EDNARVTEEUJ = 9. REJUVENATED
Made young again

10. CTRESEP =10. SPECTER
A haunting or disturbing image or prospect

11. MSONIOU =11. OMINOUS
Threatening

12. AOANDAPPRG =12. PROPAGANDA
Persuasive material put out by the advocates of a cause

13. AENTGPARO =13. PATRONAGE
Support

14. UEMATLE =14. EMULATE
To try to equal or excel through imitation

15. PETDCONEI =15. DECEPTION
A ruse; a trick

APTITUDE	Ability; talent
ARCHETYPE	An original model after which other similar things are patterned; prototype
BELEAGUERED	Harassed by; surrounded by
CANDELABRUM	A large decorative candlestick with several branches
CONFISCATED	Took
COURTING	Behaving so as to invite or incur

DECEPTION	A ruse; a trick
DISPOSITION	One's usual mood; temperament
ELOQUENT	Characterized by persuasive, powerful discourse
EMISSARY	An agent sent on a mission to represent another
EMULATE	To try to equal or excel through imitation
IMMINENT	About to happen

INTIMATED	Hinted; told privately or subtly
MARTYRED	Appeared as on who endures great suffering
MASTICATION	Chewing
MATRICULATING	Enrolling
MENAGERIE	A collection of wild animals on exhibition
NEGLIGENCE	Failure to exercise reasonable care

OMINOUS	Threatening
PATRONAGE	Support
PLEUROSIS	Illness usually occurring as a complication of pneumonia
PREPOSTEROUS	Absurd
PROPAGANDA	Persuasive material put out by the advocates of a cause
QUERULOUS	Given to complaining; peevish

REJUVENATED	Made young again
SATIRICAL	Using irony, sarcasm, or caustic wit to attack or expose folly, vice or stupidity
SLIGHTED	Made small in size, degree, or amount; lacking
SPECTER	A haunting or disturbing image or prospect
TYRANNY	Extreme harshness or severity; rigor
VESTIGE	A visible trace of something that exists no more

Glass Menagerie Vocabulary

VESTIGE	COURTING	EMISSARY	PLEUROSIS	EMULATE
MASTICATION	PATRONAGE	IMMINENT	SLIGHTED	MENAGERIE
DECEPTION	DISPOSITION	FREE SPACE	CANDELABRUM	INTIMATED
ARCHETYPE	SATIRICAL	CONFISCATED	PREPOSTEROUS	NEGLIGENCE
ELOQUENT	MARTYRED	MATRICULATING	OMINOUS	TYRANNY

Glass Menagerie Vocabulary

APTITUDE	BELEAGUERED	QUERULOUS	REJUVENATED	SPECTER
TYRANNY	OMINOUS	MATRICULATING	MARTYRED	ELOQUENT
NEGLIGENCE	PREPOSTEROUS	FREE SPACE	SATIRICAL	ARCHETYPE
INTIMATED	CANDELABRUM	PROPAGANDA	DISPOSITION	DECEPTION
MENAGERIE	SLIGHTED	IMMINENT	PATRONAGE	MASTICATION

Glass Menagerie Vocabulary

ELOQUENT	PATRONAGE	EMULATE	VESTIGE	APTITUDE
PLEUROSIS	BELEAGUERED	SATIRICAL	DISPOSITION	MATRICULATING
PROPAGANDA	MARTYRED	FREE SPACE	IMMINENT	MENAGERIE
DECEPTION	TYRANNY	SLIGHTED	CONFISCATED	MASTICATION
INTIMATED	NEGLIGENCE	CANDELABRUM	OMINOUS	ARCHETYPE

Glass Menagerie Vocabulary

PREPOSTEROUS	COURTING	REJUVENATED	EMISSARY	QUERULOUS
ARCHETYPE	OMINOUS	CANDELABRUM	NEGLIGENCE	INTIMATED
MASTICATION	CONFISCATED	FREE SPACE	TYRANNY	DECEPTION
MENAGERIE	IMMINENT	SPECTER	MARTYRED	PROPAGANDA
MATRICULATING	DISPOSITION	SATIRICAL	BELEAGUERED	PLEUROSIS

Glass Menagerie Vocabulary

SLIGHTED	TYRANNY	EMISSARY	PATRONAGE	EMULATE
SPECTER	VESTIGE	CANDELABRUM	BELEAGUERED	INTIMATED
PREPOSTEROUS	MASTICATION	FREE SPACE	SATIRICAL	ELOQUENT
COURTING	ARCHETYPE	DISPOSITION	NEGLIGENCE	PLEUROSIS
MENAGERIE	MARTYRED	OMINOUS	APTITUDE	IMMINENT

Glass Menagerie Vocabulary

QUERULOUS	PROPAGANDA	REJUVENATED	MATRICULATING	DECEPTION
IMMINENT	APTITUDE	OMINOUS	MARTYRED	MENAGERIE
PLEUROSIS	NEGLIGENCE	FREE SPACE	ARCHETYPE	COURTING
ELOQUENT	SATIRICAL	CONFISCATED	MASTICATION	PREPOSTEROUS
INTIMATED	BELEAGUERED	CANDELABRUM	VESTIGE	SPECTER

Glass Menagerie Vocabulary

EMISSARY	ELOQUENT	CANDELABRUM	DISPOSITION	PREPOSTEROUS
PLEUROSIS	PROPAGANDA	BELEAGUERED	EMULATE	SLIGHTED
ARCHETYPE	OMINOUS	FREE SPACE	SPECTER	DECEPTION
SATIRICAL	MARTYRED	VESTIGE	MASTICATION	MENAGERIE
QUERULOUS	TYRANNY	PATRONAGE	APTITUDE	COURTING

Glass Menagerie Vocabulary

NEGLIGENCE	MATRICULATING	IMMINENT	INTIMATED	CONFISCATED
COURTING	APTITUDE	PATRONAGE	TYRANNY	QUERULOUS
MENAGERIE	MASTICATION	FREE SPACE	MARTYRED	SATIRICAL
DECEPTION	SPECTER	REJUVENATED	OMINOUS	ARCHETYPE
SLIGHTED	EMULATE	BELEAGUERED	PROPAGANDA	PLEUROSIS

Glass Menagerie Vocabulary

SATIRICAL	TYRANNY	SLIGHTED	DECEPTION	IMMINENT
DISPOSITION	MENAGERIE	PLEUROSIS	EMISSARY	REJUVENATED
PROPAGANDA	SPECTER	FREE SPACE	OMINOUS	PATRONAGE
CANDELABRUM	ELOQUENT	MASTICATION	QUERULOUS	CONFISCATED
COURTING	VESTIGE	MATRICULATING	BELEAGUERED	NEGLIGENCE

Glass Menagerie Vocabulary

MARTYRED	PREPOSTEROUS	EMULATE	ARCHETYPE	APTITUDE
NEGLIGENCE	BELEAGUERED	MATRICULATING	VESTIGE	COURTING
CONFISCATED	QUERULOUS	FREE SPACE	ELOQUENT	CANDELABRUM
PATRONAGE	OMINOUS	INTIMATED	SPECTER	PROPAGANDA
REJUVENATED	EMISSARY	PLEUROSIS	MENAGERIE	DISPOSITION

Glass Menagerie Vocabulary

TYRANNY	OMINOUS	ELOQUENT	SLIGHTED	IMMINENT
PROPAGANDA	EMULATE	PREPOSTEROUS	VESTIGE	CANDELABRUM
SPECTER	REJUVENATED	FREE SPACE	INTIMATED	MASTICATION
MENAGERIE	MATRICULATING	APTITUDE	COURTING	DECEPTION
PLEUROSIS	SATIRICAL	CONFISCATED	PATRONAGE	NEGLIGENCE

Glass Menagerie Vocabulary

EMISSARY	DISPOSITION	BELEAGUERED	ARCHETYPE	MARTYRED
NEGLIGENCE	PATRONAGE	CONFISCATED	SATIRICAL	PLEUROSIS
DECEPTION	COURTING	FREE SPACE	MATRICULATING	MENAGERIE
MASTICATION	INTIMATED	QUERULOUS	REJUVENATED	SPECTER
CANDELABRUM	VESTIGE	PREPOSTEROUS	EMULATE	PROPAGANDA

Glass Menagerie Vocabulary

SPECTER	PATRONAGE	MATRICULATING	SATIRICAL	PREPOSTEROUS
IMMINENT	EMULATE	SLIGHTED	NEGLIGENCE	COURTING
DECEPTION	OMINOUS	FREE SPACE	MARTYRED	ELOQUENT
ARCHETYPE	DISPOSITION	CONFISCATED	MENAGERIE	TYRANNY
INTIMATED	PROPAGANDA	APTITUDE	BELEAGUERED	EMISSARY

Glass Menagerie Vocabulary

VESTIGE	CANDELABRUM	QUERULOUS	PLEUROSIS	REJUVENATED
EMISSARY	BELEAGUERED	APTITUDE	PROPAGANDA	INTIMATED
TYRANNY	MENAGERIE	FREE SPACE	DISPOSITION	ARCHETYPE
ELOQUENT	MARTYRED	MASTICATION	OMINOUS	DECEPTION
COURTING	NEGLIGENCE	SLIGHTED	EMULATE	IMMINENT

Glass Menagerie Vocabulary

BELEAGUERED	MATRICULATING	VESTIGE	PLEUROSIS	ELOQUENT
EMULATE	REJUVENATED	DISPOSITION	PROPAGANDA	APTITUDE
ARCHETYPE	QUERULOUS	FREE SPACE	CONFISCATED	TYRANNY
COURTING	OMINOUS	PATRONAGE	SLIGHTED	NEGLIGENCE
EMISSARY	IMMINENT	MENAGERIE	CANDELABRUM	DECEPTION

Glass Menagerie Vocabulary

PREPOSTEROUS	MARTYRED	MASTICATION	SPECTER	INTIMATED
DECEPTION	CANDELABRUM	MENAGERIE	IMMINENT	EMISSARY
NEGLIGENCE	SLIGHTED	FREE SPACE	OMINOUS	COURTING
TYRANNY	CONFISCATED	SATIRICAL	QUERULOUS	ARCHETYPE
APTITUDE	PROPAGANDA	DISPOSITION	REJUVENATED	EMULATE

Glass Menagerie Vocabulary

MASTICATION	MATRICULATING	PLEUROSIS	OMINOUS	APTITUDE
PREPOSTEROUS	IMMINENT	COURTING	QUERULOUS	BELEAGUERED
CANDELABRUM	SLIGHTED	FREE SPACE	TYRANNY	MENAGERIE
DISPOSITION	SATIRICAL	ARCHETYPE	EMULATE	SPECTER
PATRONAGE	EMISSARY	PROPAGANDA	VESTIGE	CONFISCATED

Glass Menagerie Vocabulary

NEGLIGENCE	MARTYRED	REJUVENATED	DECEPTION	INTIMATED
CONFISCATED	VESTIGE	PROPAGANDA	EMISSARY	PATRONAGE
SPECTER	EMULATE	FREE SPACE	SATIRICAL	DISPOSITION
MENAGERIE	TYRANNY	ELOQUENT	SLIGHTED	CANDELABRUM
BELEAGUERED	QUERULOUS	COURTING	IMMINENT	PREPOSTEROUS

Glass Menagerie Vocabulary

SATIRICAL	IMMINENT	NEGLIGENCE	SLIGHTED	PLEUROSIS
MARTYRED	MASTICATION	DISPOSITION	QUERULOUS	ELOQUENT
INTIMATED	PROPAGANDA	FREE SPACE	CANDELABRUM	SPECTER
VESTIGE	APTITUDE	EMISSARY	MATRICULATING	ARCHETYPE
OMINOUS	COURTING	REJUVENATED	EMULATE	MENAGERIE

Glass Menagerie Vocabulary

PATRONAGE	TYRANNY	DECEPTION	CONFISCATED	BELEAGUERED
MENAGERIE	EMULATE	REJUVENATED	COURTING	OMINOUS
ARCHETYPE	MATRICULATING	FREE SPACE	APTITUDE	VESTIGE
SPECTER	CANDELABRUM	PREPOSTEROUS	PROPAGANDA	INTIMATED
ELOQUENT	QUERULOUS	DISPOSITION	MASTICATION	MARTYRED

Glass Menagerie Vocabulary

CONFISCATED	PREPOSTEROUS	COURTING	APTITUDE	ELOQUENT
SLIGHTED	ARCHETYPE	IMMINENT	PROPAGANDA	EMISSARY
MATRICULATING	OMINOUS	FREE SPACE	DECEPTION	REJUVENATED
SATIRICAL	BELEAGUERED	NEGLIGENCE	VESTIGE	INTIMATED
PATRONAGE	MASTICATION	MARTYRED	SPECTER	EMULATE

Glass Menagerie Vocabulary

MENAGERIE	DISPOSITION	PLEUROSIS	QUERULOUS	TYRANNY
EMULATE	SPECTER	MARTYRED	MASTICATION	PATRONAGE
INTIMATED	VESTIGE	FREE SPACE	BELEAGUERED	SATIRICAL
REJUVENATED	DECEPTION	CANDELABRUM	OMINOUS	MATRICULATING
EMISSARY	PROPAGANDA	IMMINENT	ARCHETYPE	SLIGHTED

Glass Menagerie Vocabulary

MATRICULATING	DISPOSITION	COURTING	ELOQUENT	PATRONAGE
CANDELABRUM	DECEPTION	REJUVENATED	APTITUDE	BELEAGUERED
SATIRICAL	EMISSARY	FREE SPACE	MASTICATION	OMINOUS
TYRANNY	QUERULOUS	EMULATE	IMMINENT	NEGLIGENCE
ARCHETYPE	SPECTER	PLEUROSIS	PREPOSTEROUS	SLIGHTED

Glass Menagerie Vocabulary

VESTIGE	CONFISCATED	MENAGERIE	INTIMATED	PROPAGANDA
SLIGHTED	PREPOSTEROUS	PLEUROSIS	SPECTER	ARCHETYPE
NEGLIGENCE	IMMINENT	FREE SPACE	QUERULOUS	TYRANNY
OMINOUS	MASTICATION	MARTYRED	EMISSARY	SATIRICAL
BELEAGUERED	APTITUDE	REJUVENATED	DECEPTION	CANDELABRUM

Glass Menagerie Vocabulary

INTIMATED	CANDELABRUM	NEGLIGENCE	BELEAGUERED	MARTYRED
REJUVENATED	COURTING	CONFISCATED	EMULATE	DECEPTION
VESTIGE	ELOQUENT	FREE SPACE	PLEUROSIS	TYRANNY
PROPAGANDA	PATRONAGE	OMINOUS	ARCHETYPE	DISPOSITION
QUERULOUS	PREPOSTEROUS	MENAGERIE	SLIGHTED	IMMINENT

Glass Menagerie Vocabulary

SATIRICAL	APTITUDE	MATRICULATING	EMISSARY	MASTICATION
IMMINENT	SLIGHTED	MENAGERIE	PREPOSTEROUS	QUERULOUS
DISPOSITION	ARCHETYPE	FREE SPACE	PATRONAGE	PROPAGANDA
TYRANNY	PLEUROSIS	SPECTER	ELOQUENT	VESTIGE
DECEPTION	EMULATE	CONFISCATED	COURTING	REJUVENATED

Glass Menagerie Vocabulary

EMULATE	PROPAGANDA	REJUVENATED	SPECTER	CONFISCATED
TYRANNY	SATIRICAL	MARTYRED	CANDELABRUM	APTITUDE
BELEAGUERED	NEGLIGENCE	FREE SPACE	IMMINENT	EMISSARY
MENAGERIE	SLIGHTED	ELOQUENT	DECEPTION	PREPOSTEROUS
COURTING	VESTIGE	INTIMATED	MATRICULATING	PATRONAGE

Glass Menagerie Vocabulary

OMINOUS	ARCHETYPE	MASTICATION	DISPOSITION	QUERULOUS
PATRONAGE	MATRICULATING	INTIMATED	VESTIGE	COURTING
PREPOSTEROUS	DECEPTION	FREE SPACE	SLIGHTED	MENAGERIE
EMISSARY	IMMINENT	PLEUROSIS	NEGLIGENCE	BELEAGUERED
APTITUDE	CANDELABRUM	MARTYRED	SATIRICAL	TYRANNY

Glass Menagerie Vocabulary

REJUVENATED	BELEAGUERED	PATRONAGE	SPECTER	EMISSARY
EMULATE	TYRANNY	PREPOSTEROUS	SATIRICAL	SLIGHTED
OMINOUS	ELOQUENT	FREE SPACE	DISPOSITION	VESTIGE
CONFISCATED	QUERULOUS	NEGLIGENCE	PLEUROSIS	ARCHETYPE
APTITUDE	INTIMATED	IMMINENT	CANDELABRUM	DECEPTION

Glass Menagerie Vocabulary

MARTYRED	COURTING	MASTICATION	PROPAGANDA	MATRICULATING
DECEPTION	CANDELABRUM	IMMINENT	INTIMATED	APTITUDE
ARCHETYPE	PLEUROSIS	FREE SPACE	QUERULOUS	CONFISCATED
VESTIGE	DISPOSITION	MENAGERIE	ELOQUENT	OMINOUS
SLIGHTED	SATIRICAL	PREPOSTEROUS	TYRANNY	EMULATE

Glass Menagerie Vocabulary

EMULATE	CONFISCATED	SATIRICAL	ELOQUENT	SLIGHTED
MENAGERIE	ARCHETYPE	PATRONAGE	IMMINENT	QUERULOUS
PLEUROSIS	CANDELABRUM	FREE SPACE	REJUVENATED	MASTICATION
EMISSARY	PROPAGANDA	MATRICULATING	SPECTER	DECEPTION
VESTIGE	OMINOUS	MARTYRED	DISPOSITION	APTITUDE

Glass Menagerie Vocabulary

PREPOSTEROUS	BELEAGUERED	INTIMATED	COURTING	TYRANNY
APTITUDE	DISPOSITION	MARTYRED	OMINOUS	VESTIGE
DECEPTION	SPECTER	FREE SPACE	PROPAGANDA	EMISSARY
MASTICATION	REJUVENATED	NEGLIGENCE	CANDELABRUM	PLEUROSIS
QUERULOUS	IMMINENT	PATRONAGE	ARCHETYPE	MENAGERIE

www.ingramcontent.com/pod-product-compliance
Lightning Source LLC
Chambersburg PA
CBHW081458070526
44586CB00019B/2411